T0149247

A Real Kingdom
Is Coming!

Truths about the Kingdom of God

Israel Marrone

WESTBOW
PRESS®
A DIVISION OF THOMAS NELSON
& ZONDERVAN

Scripture taken from the King James Version of the Bible.

Scripture taken from the New King James Version. Copyright © 1979, 1980, 1982 by Thomas Nelson, Inc. Used by permission. All rights reserved.

Scripture taken from the *Amplified Bible*, copyright © 1954, 1958, 1962, 1964, 1965, 1987 by The Lockman Foundation. Used by permission.

WestBow Press books may be ordered through booksellers or by contacting:

WestBow Press
A Division of Thomas Nelson & Zondervan
1663 Liberty Drive
Bloomington, IN 47403
www.westbowpress.com
1 (866) 928-1240

ISBN: 978-1-5127-2564-3 (sc)
ISBN: 978-1-5127-2565-0 (hc)
ISBN: 978-1-5127-2563-6 (e)

Library of Congress Control Number: 2016900071

Print information available on the last page.

WestBow Press rev. date: 1/27/2016

Contents

Acknowledgments

From My Heart

While I was writing this book, my instruction from the Holy Spirit was straightforward indeed: "Write only what I have inspired you to write, and don't let your traditions get in the way." Whether you agree with me, debate with me, or join me in understanding the kingdom of God, I'll present you with everything I've been given. I have based every word, thought, and concept on the Scriptures God's infallible Word. My experience with the kingdom of God has involved exhaustive research, inspiration, and actual experience.

I'm eternally grateful to Jesus Christ for extending his hand of righteousness and salvation. I'm thankful for the baptism of the Holy Spirit and every gift God has given me. I love God with all my heart, mind, and soul. I am nothing without God, Jesus Christ, and the Holy Spirit.

Over fifteen years ago, when I was first inspired to write this book, I had no idea I'd be challenged, massive chaos would break loose, and I'd be attacked by the kingdom of darkness. After battling alcoholism, adultery, and iniquity, I can truly say I am now clean by the grace of God. My family is still intact. Shanda, my lovely wife of thirty-three years, is still with me, and our marriage is stronger than ever. God had to completely clean me up and rid me of all sin and iniquity before I could take on this monumental task. This is why I now understand this book is so valuable to the body of Christ.

My heart goes out to every apostle, prophet, evangelist, pastor, and teacher God has given assignments to only to find out the moment they said yes that they would experience firsthand much opposition from the other side.

I express my sincere appreciation to my dad, the late Nathaniel Brown, and my mom, Curlene. They raised me the right way with strong morals and a love for God. As long as I can remember, they took me to Sunday school and kept me actively involved in every aspect of church fellowship.

I thank the late bishop Walter Hawkins for all the conversations and study of the kingdom of God we had. Thank you, Bishop John Carlton White, presiding prelate of the Church of God in Christ International. He saw something in me in 2002 and consecrated me to the sacred office of bishop.

I acknowledge my spiritual father, the late Bishop Martin Jefferson Clifton, for constantly teaching, training, and pouring into me. He let me know I could do anything but fail.

I will be forever grateful to Bishop Jessie Dickens, prelate of the California Western Ecclesiastical Jurisdiction Church of God in Christ. Bishop Jessie Dickens, a man of great integrity and holiness, taught me the expression of being nothing but "dirt" and how to live a holy and separated life by example.

I thank God for forgiving and forgetting my sins and teaching me to forgive myself.

I thank Prophet Terrell Turner, who came into my life as I struggled with my identity and writing this book. The prophet spoke into my life and gave me the motivation to hear from God and write.

This book wouldn't have been possible without the patience and prayers of the saints at Alllove Faith Church of God in Christ, International in Antioch and Oakland, California. I thank God for my faithful and committed administration staff—Tamika Peters, Pastor Georgia Peters, Decynthia Henderson, Brother Leroy Bellamy, and Brother Leonard Stephens, president of OURTV. I thank God for the intercessory prayer group—Elder Richard Strong, Irdean Watson, and Geraldine Ashley, and the board of CPEJ COGIC International, Bishop-Elect Earl Roberson, Bishop Mario Gaines, Bishop Sir Winston, and Bishop Ignacio Pajarillo.

I also thank the love of my life, Shanda. Unlike other women who have been cheated on, she constantly prayed for me every morning at five. She was faithful and continued to speak words of faith of the greatness God had in store for me.

To all my children, who love me unconditionally, I say, "Thanks a million."

—Israel Marrone

Preface

Inspired by God

There is a real kingdom coming quite soon. This kingdom is not an imaginary, ethereal concept but an actual kingdom that dwells presently in the invisible but will soon take on physical embodiment. This kingdom has a real King, a domain, and subjects.

The Holy Spirit inspired this book. I received an assignment from the throne of God to educate, motivate, and encourage others to spread the gospel of the kingdom of God. This subject was chosen because it was the central theme of the teaching of Jesus Christ.

My main motivation in writing this book was to restore the integrity of the teaching of Jesus Christ and to bring it to the forefront again.

I'll give you a description of what the kingdom of God is, who the present King is, and biblical prophecy concerning this kingdom. By God's grace, I'll offer the reason for the tragedy that this message of Jesus Christ has gone missing in the modern church.

I'll address the statement of Jesus Christ when he said the "Kingdom of God comes with power." (Mark 9:1 KJV) (1Corinthians 4:20) I will settle scripturally the ageless debate about where the kingdom of God is and the distinction between the church and the kingdom. I will answer the question of how we can seek the kingdom of God and address the controversial subject of dying and going to heaven.

I began my research, development, and outlining for this book in 2002, but 2006 through 2009 were my darkest hours of trials and tribulations. The years 2010 through 2013 were my years of development and 2014 was the year of my restoration and release. It was necessary for me to go through several trials and test so that I would be able to understand the realness of the kingdom of God. I discovered how to walk in authority and in the now in God's kingdom.

I had a one-on-one encounter with the invisible world and the seen world. I will never forget the loud, thunderous noise in my ear as I lay in bed with my wife, Shanda, only to later find out it was angels.

You will feel a strong sense of the presence of God as you read this book, and it will reveal many mysteries. I will address age-old questions of the existence of God and his kingdom.

Every time Jesus Christ taught or preached the gospel of the kingdom of God, his words were confirmed in the manifestation of healing, deliverance, salvation, miracles, and divine encounters with God.

Be prayerful and consider the purpose and intent of Jesus Christ's teaching and preaching the gospel of the kingdom of God.

Introduction

What Do We Expect?

In 1983, just before being ordained a minister in the Church of God in Christ by the late Bishop German Reed Ross, I met with him while fishing in Tracy, California. New candidates were required to have personal interviews with their bishop before being ordained so he could get a feel for where their hearts were and to receive final instruction prior to ordination.

At the end of the interview, he asked me if I had any questions. Here was the highly respected general secretary of the church giving me the opportunity to ask him any question, and one came to mind. I was learning about Jesus' second coming and his kingdom being established on earth. I asked the bishop his opinion of one-world government if it were in the hands of humanity. He had a perplexed look on his face; his answer was immediate and emphatic: "Now just keep your mind on Jesus, son. Those matters are too great for you." After seeing my sincerity, he explained that the church was the kingdom of God and the government would eventually be led by the church.

That made a lasting impression on me. I've never forgotten that conversation with him that took place over thirty years ago. Since then, many forward thinkers have suggested that one-world government is the only way to preserve humanity. But many questions arise. Who would establish it? How would it be implemented? What laws would it administer? How would they be enforced? Would sovereign nations relinquish their authority to it? Would it succeed, or would it eventually oppress and enslave all humanity? These questions always stop thinkers, planners, leaders, and scientists in their tracks. Years later, God has given me a deeper revelation into this subject.

Why are we not preaching what Jesus preached? Is the message Jesus spent his ministry on dated? We hear about prosperity, salvation, healing, miracles, deliverance, and even social well-being, which are all by-products of the kingdom of God.

The ministry of Jesus Christ began by his saying, "Repent for the kingdom of Heaven is at hand" (Matthew 4:17 KJV). He traveled to teach and preach the gospel of the kingdom of God (Luke 8:1 GW) It's startling to realize the central theme of Jesus' teaching, the gospel of the kingdom of God, has become conspicuously missing from the church. Those who are carriers of the gospel have made the main teaching of Jesus obsolete. We have the responsibility to resurrect this profound teaching of Jesus and herald it over the airwaves and from the pulpits. Jesus said, "and this gospel of the kingdom shall be preached in all the world for a witness unto all nations; and then shall the end come." (Matthew 24:14 KJV). The good news equates to this: this world system shall end, but the kingdom of God shall begin to reign and rule.

In this book, I will define why this teaching of Jesus Christ was so important then and now. By the leading of the Holy Spirit, I will also establish what this kingdom does for the believer now and how we can all become a part of the kingdom of God. I thank God for all my trials and tests I went through after this was conceived in my spirit over thirty years ago. God told me to write, but I made every excuse to avoid doing so because I knew the great price I would have to pay.

My Personal Belief: The Apostles' Creed

I believe in God the Father Almighty, Maker of heaven and earth. And in Jesus Christ his only Son, our Lord, who was conceived by the Holy Ghost, born of the Virgin Mary, suffered under Pontius Pilate, was crucified, dead, and buried; he descended into hell; the third day he rose again from the dead; he ascended into heaven, and sitteth on the right hand of God the Father Almighty; from thence he shall come to judge the quick and the dead.

I believe in the Holy Ghost, the holy church, the communion of saints, the forgiveness of sins, the resurrection of the body, and the life everlasting, amen.

Chapter 1

What Is the Kingdom of God?

From that time Jesus began to preach and to say,
"Repent, for the kingdom of heaven is at hand."
—Matthew 4:17 (KJV)

Jesus heralded the message "Repent." If you want to repent, you'll need to turn from sin and change your life. *To repent* means to feel regret or contrition for your ways, to have a change of heart or mind. When you repent, you'll turn to the person who told you to repent in the first place and develop a new way of thinking that includes the kingdom of God.

The Hebrew word for *kingdom* is *malkut,* and its Greek counterpart is *basileia.*[1] Both terms primarily mean "rule" or "reign." Only secondarily do they denote a realm, sphere, or territory over which a rule or reign is exercised. Both terms have a dynamic, active meaning and refer to the exercise of God's power, dominion, or sovereignty. This is clear in the Old Testament, particularly in the poetry of the Psalms, where parallel lines clarify what the word *kingdom* means. Psalm 22:28 says, "For the kingdom is the

---

[1] W. E. Vines, *Expository Dictionary of New Testament Words,* 1940.

Lord's, and He rules over all." Similarly, Psalm 103:19 states, "The Lord has established His throne [kingdom] in the heavens, and His sovereignty rules over all." Psalm 145:11 declares, "They shall speak of the glory of Thy kingdom, and talk of Thy power." Here, kingdom is associated with the ideas of God's rule, sovereignty, and power.

The New Testament term means the same thing. When we pray, "Thy kingdom come, Thy will be done, on earth, as it is in heaven" (Matthew 6:10), we're asking God to exert His authority in the world so his purposes will be achieved. In Jesus' parable about "A certain nobleman who went to a distant country to receive a kingdom," those over whom he was to rule said, "We do not want this man to reign over us" (Luke 19:12, 14). Paul taught that redemption amounted to an exchange of rulers over our lives; he wrote "who hath delivered us from the power of darkness, and hath translated us into the kingdom of his dear Son." The New Testament nuance for "kingdom" in these verses connects it with the exertion of God's will, the act of ruling or reigning, the exercise of authority. So the expression "kingdom of God" doesn't refer to heaven, the church, the heart, moral reform, or a future realm. Rather, it refers to the active, dynamic exercise of God's rule, authority, dominion, and power in the world.

The kingdom of God is the presence, goodness, and power of God. It's God's way of doing things, his profound reign and rule over everything everywhere. We have witnessed much debate over this "kingdom of God" matter. The preaching and teaching on this subject have been lost through centuries of controversial interpretations of it. Most leaders today equate the kingdom of God as a Christian church while others have avoided the subject entirely. But if we don't have a basic understanding of something, we'll tend not to discuss it for fear of implying the wrong thing. Even I had avoided this subject, but after much prayer and contemplation, I believe the Holy Spirit released me to write this treatise.

A kingdom has a person of authority who leads it, and every kingdom has a territory, its domain. The most important aspect of any construction project is the foundation. If it's done incorrect or if it's not plumb, the project is heading for disaster. A kingdom is a country, state, or territory ruled by a king or queen, but it is also the spiritual reign and authority of God. In both instances, the king is the dominating authority.

The king is an absolute, supreme ruler, a monarch. His authority and ability to govern resides in a single person. This style is not a form of government familiar to most of us. During the summer of 2013, I was intrigued by the series *The White Queen* on television; I saw the complete authority of the king in all matters; he had the final say. The buck ended with the king, the monarch, who alone possessed supreme power in the kingdom. We find the concept of a monarchy in the New Testament, which has a direct connection with the future of humanity. Jesus continually taught and preached the gospel of the kingdom, the central theme of his message.

As we read in Matthew 6:9–13, Jesus Christ was a model for people who wanted to learn how to pray effectively. Most people know this passage as the Lord's Prayer but may not have considered it carefully. In it, Jesus referred to the kingdom of God, he pleaded for it to come, and he acknowledged it was God's by declaring, "Thine is the kingdom." When we acknowledge God's kingdom, we acknowledge he is almighty. Scripture shows that the kingdom of God is yet to come; when it does, the world will witness an obvious and dramatic event, but few people who preach about this kingdom believe this. Few even acknowledge the word *kingdom* except in an ethereal sense. What does the Bible have to say about the kingdom of God?

The Kingdom Theme in the Gospels

Jesus Christ spoke about the kingdom of heaven in the gospel of Matthew. He taught about the kingdom of God on several occasions in the other three gospels—Mark, Luke, and John. To help us better understand the concept of the kingdom of God, I'll give you this definition from the *Moody Handbook of Theology*.[2] While many believe the kingdom of God and kingdom of heaven refer to different things, both phrases refer to the same thing. The phrase "kingdom of God" occurred sixty-eight times in ten New Testament books, while "kingdom of heaven" occurs only thirty-two times and only in the gospel of Matthew. Based on Matthew's exclusive use of the phrase and the Jewish nature of his gospel, some interpreters have concluded that Matthew was writing concerning the millennial kingdom while the other New Testament authors were referring to the universal kingdom. However, a closer study of the use of the phrase reveals that this interpretation is in error.

For example, speaking to the rich young ruler, Christ used "kingdom of heaven" and "kingdom of God" interchangeably. "Then Jesus said to his disciples, 'I tell you the truth, it is hard for a rich man to enter the kingdom of heaven'" (Matthew 19:23). In the next verse, Christ proclaimed, "Again I tell you, it is easier for a camel to go through the eye of a needle than for a rich man to enter the kingdom of God" (v. 24). Jesus made no distinction between the two terms; he seemed to consider them synonymous.

Mark and Luke used "kingdom of God." Matthew used "kingdom of heaven" frequently in parallel accounts of the same parable. Compare Matthew 11:11–12 with Luke 7:28; Matthew 13:11 with Mark 4:11 and Luke 8:10; Matthew 13:24 with Mark 4:26; Matthew

---

[2] "Paul Ens, The Moody Handbook of Theology (Chicago: Moody Publishers, 1989)."

13:31 with Mark 4:30 and Luke 13:18; Matthew 13:33 with Luke 13:20; Matthew 18:3 with Mark 10:14 and Luke 18:16; and Matthew 22:2. In each instance, Matthew used the phrase "kingdom of heaven" while Mark and Luke used "kingdom of God." Clearly, the two phrases refer to the same thing.

The Kingdom of God in Power

We must think in terms of the kingdom of God being able to demonstrate his power and authority. When Jesus was casting out devils in Matthew 12:28 (Weymouth New Testament), he said, "But if it is by the power of the Spirit of God that I expel the demons, it is evident that the kingdom of God has come upon you." On another occasion, when Jesus was giving his disciples their marching orders for campaigns to other cities, he said, "and heal the sick there, and say to them, 'The Kingdom of God has come near you'" (Luke 10:9 NKJV). When the kingdom of God comes upon you in a demonstration of God's power, demons and devils don't stand a chance because they are ultimately subject to a higher authority, the Spirit of God. Sickness and disease are no match for the kingdom of God. That's powerful!

When the kingdom of God comes upon you, everything comes into divine order instantaneously. The kingdom of God coming near you will rid you of sickness and disease. This message has been lost through time because of satanic influences in the world today. Every time the gospel of the kingdom of God was preached, demons were cast out and the sick were healed.

The Enemy has influenced today's leaders to preach and teach parts of the gospel of the kingdom but not others. Due to denominational influences, many leaders focus on the fringe benefits of the gospel of the kingdom based on tradition.

The gospel became diluted and indigenous of the kingdom of darkness.

Let me qualify this statement with two passages from Scripture. Mark 7:13 (ISV) states, "You are destroying the word of God through your tradition that you have handed down. So you do many other things like that." Colossians 2:8 states, "Beware lest any man spoil you through philosophy and vain deceit, after the tradition of men, after the rudiments of the world and not after Christ."

My preaching style was always precise. I never allowed my opinion or thoughts to distort God's Word. I'll do the same here and let the Scriptures do what they were designed to do. When we return to preaching and teaching the true gospel of the kingdom as Jesus did, we'll start seeing the same results Jesus did; he stated, "Truly, I tell all of you emphatically, the one who believes in me will also do what I'm doing. He will do even greater things than these, because I'm going to the Father" (John 14:12 ISV).

The Kingdom of God—God's Way of Doing Things

The kingdom of God is his way of making things we can't comprehend actually come about. A seed planted and watered can bring forth a harvest many times greater than the seed itself.

After hearing that John the Baptist had been beheaded, Jesus withdrew to a solitary place, but the crowds followed him there. When Jesus saw the crowd, he had compassion on them and healed the sick. As evening approached, Jesus' disciples told him that because they were in a remote place with no food, Jesus should tell them to go home.

Jesus refused to send them away; the Son of God seized this opportunity to show the people firsthand God's way of doing things. Little is much in the kingdom of God! Jesus instructed the disciples to bring what they had to him—five loaves of bread and two fish. Jesus looked to heaven, gave thanks, and broke the loaves. He gave the food to the disciples to serve five thousand, not counting the women and children, though they weren't enough to serve even one family. Afterward, they had twelve baskets of leftovers. Praise God!

The kingdom of God multiplied what was available to satisfy the need of a multitude. The kingdom of God has ways of changing outcomes for God to be glorified. The kingdom of God can increase and decrease as the need arises. When you "Seek first the kingdom of God all things that are needed will be added," that is powerful! Every kingdom has a king, and it's no different with the kingdom of God.

The Throne

> The LORD has established His throne in heaven,
> and His kingdom rules over all.
> —Psalm 103:19 NKJV

The Lord of any kingdom has power and authority over others. In the kingdom of God, the Lord is the almighty God in the person of God the Father, God the Son, and God the Holy Spirit. David, who was credited with writing the Psalms, knew kings and kingdoms; he was the anointed king of Israel who had taken over the kingdom after God had rejected King Saul. King David was the lord of Israel's armies. The Lord always carried out the wishes of the king and the kingdom. In this case, the Lord, God Almighty in three persons, established his throne in heaven, and the throne of any kingdom is its seat of authority.

John, who wrote Revelation, experienced the throne of God. In Revelation 4, as he approached heaven, John saw a door standing open. If the sky was like an open window to Jesus at his baptism (Mark 1:10–11), it was like an open door to John. A voice, the trumpet-like voice he had heard once before, beckoned him to take a spiritual ride through the doorway. The voice told him to come and see what was to come to pass after that.

John stopped short of narrating a full-blown heavenly excursion as had Enoch in Jewish literature and Paul, who was "caught up to the third heaven" and "heard inexpressible things, things that man is not allowed to reveal" (2 Corinthians 12:2, 4). All John wrote was that he had been in the essence of the spirit, just as in the introductory vision on Patmos (Revelation 1:10). There, he was "in the essence of the spirit" first and then heard the voice; here, it was the other way around. Nowhere have we been told when or under what factors John stopped being "in the essence of the Spirit," but we are told he was in the essence of the Spirit again. That time, he was really caught up to heaven, for he saw an occupied throne. Only to a restricted degree can we attain in our reading of Revelation a sense of where John was.

John's recount of what he saw in heaven is, as is the rest of the Word of God, true to the classic Jewish standard that "no one has ever glimpsed at God" (John 1:18; 1 John 4:12) as we draw a comparison with Ezekiel 33:2. In numerous ways, it recalls Ezekiel's introductory dream in Ezekiel 1:4–28, except that John was even more reluctant than Ezekiel about naming or describing God exactly. What John saw was a throne room and a temple. Ezekiel glimpsed a throne of sapphire. "And above the firmament over their heads was the likeness of a throne, in appearance like a sapphire stone; on the likeness of the throne *was* a likeness with the appearance of a man high above it" (Ezekiel 1:26). He recognized "the look of the likeness of the glory of the Lord" (1:28). John, by contrast, wrote only of a throne in paradise and somebody seated on it. He did not name who it was; he wrote just that someone sat there with the appearance of jasper and carnelian.

To John, the throne showed the power and majesty of the Almighty sitting on the throne. The significance of jasper, a stone of many colors, and carnelian, a hard, red chalcedony used in jewelry, gives a glimpse of the power of the throne and the one who sat on it. John saw everything else in relation to the throne. He saw a rainbow that resembled an emerald. The rainbow was significant because it showed the throne's representation of all nations, and the emerald demonstrated how precious these nations were to God.

Surrounding the throne were twenty-four other thrones on which were seated elders in white who wore gold crowns. From it came flashes of lightning, rumbling, and peals of thunder. Seven lights were blazing in front of it; John recognized these as the seven spirits of God, which we will find significant in the rule of the kingdom of God. He glimpsed what looked like a sea of glass, clear as crystal. In the center, around the throne, John glimpsed four animals with eyes on every edge and six wings who constantly said, "Holy, holy, holy is the Lord God Almighty, who was, and is, and is to arrive."

John's experience, having begun as a fantastic picture unfolding step by step before John's eyes, became a view of ongoing worship and praise. The use of verbs in the present tense beginning in verse 5 and the saying "day and night" in verse 8, suggest it wasn't a singular incident but an ongoing ritual in paradise. The creatures were hailing the anonymous someone seated on it as the Lord God Almighty (compare Revelation 1:8). In answer, the twenty-four elders continually dropped down to worship the one who lived for ever and ever, laying their crests in front of the throne and saying, "You are worthy, our Lord and God, to receive glory and respect and power, for you conceived all things, and by your will they were conceived and have their being." The elders' recital celebrated creation and God the Creator.

The Seven Spirits of God

The seven spirits of God in John's spiritual encounter with heaven are significant in God's reign and rule in the spiritual realm, the realm of the unseen. Two worlds are in simultaneous existence—the seen world or physical world, and the unseen world or spiritual world. Why is this significant? Paul discussed this realm like this: "while we look not at the things which are seen, but at the things which are not seen: for the things which are seen *are* temporal; but the things which are not seen *are* eternal" (2 Corinthians 4:18 KJV).

The things of the physical world are temporal; the kingdom of God is eternal. I will explain the significance of the seven spirits so you can draw things out of the unseen world into the physical realm through reliance on the kingdom of God. Once you determine how things are done and how things are brought to you, nothing will be withheld from you. I know these things because they are proven. I exercise them daily. I'm often asked how I do certain things that are seemingly impossible for humans to do; I say it's because of the kingdom of God. I'm most often greeted with perplexed looks, but I'll refer to this Scripture repeatedly because it's true.

Jesus said, "He that believeth on me, the works that I do shall he do also; and greater *works* than these shall he do; because I go unto my Father" (John 14:12). Actually, when he said, "I go unto my Father," he meant, "I am going to the realm where the kingdom of God reigns and rules." In Matthew 9:29–30, when Jesus went into the dwelling, the blind men asked to be healed, and Jesus asked them, "'Do you accept as true that I am able to do this?' They said to him, 'Yes, Lord.' Then he affected their eyes, saying, 'According to your belief be it finished to you.' And their eyes were opened. And Jesus sternly alerted them, 'See that no one knows about it.'" What we consider impossible becomes possible through our reliance on the kingdom of God.

Before Jesus prayed or performed anything, the kingdom of God needed to sanction it, a vital requirement. If you want results, the kingdom of God will have to sanction it. He asked them, "Do you accept as true that I am able to do this?" If they hadn't first accepted that the kingdom of God could override their circumstances, it wouldn't have happened. The moment they said, "Yes, Lord," the kingdom of God opened their eyes. Jesus sealed the action of the kingdom of God when he said, "According to your faith be it done unto you." What Jesus meant was, "According to your belief (seeing it as done or complete) be it finished to you."

Have you ever wondered what the seven spirits of God were? Several years ago, while I was fasting and listening to God's Spirit, I began to discern several Scriptures that I had read before but hadn't sought any spiritual insight from.

- Revelation 3:1 (NKJV): "And to the angel of the church in Sardis write, 'These things says He who has the seven Spirits of God and the seven stars: "I know your works, that you have a name that you are alive, but you are dead."'"
- Revelation 3:6 (NKJV): "He who has an ear, let him hear what the Spirit says to the churches."
- Revelation 4:5 (NKJV): "And from the throne proceeded lightning's, thundering's, and voices. Seven lamps of fire *were* burning before the throne, which are the seven Spirits of God."

- Revelation 5:6: "And I looked, and behold, in the midst of the throne and of the four living creatures, and in the midst of the elders, stood a Lamb as though it had been slain, having seven horns and seven eyes, which are the seven Spirits of God sent out into all the earth."

After reading these Scriptures, I realized Jesus had these seven spirits, which are the eyes of the Lord represented by the seven lamps or lampstands of fire. We will also find this same revelation by the prophet Zechariah.

- Zechariah 4:2 (NKJV): "And he said to me, 'What do you see?' So I said, 'I am looking, and there *is* a lampstand of solid gold with a bowl on top of it, and on the stand seven lamps with seven pipes to the seven lamps.'"
- Zechariah 4:6 (NKJV): "So he answered and said to me: 'This *is* the word of the Lord to Zerubbabel: "Not by might nor by power, but by My Spirit," Says the Lord of hosts.'"

Zechariah 4:10 tells us that these seven lamps were the eyes of the Lord. This agrees with Revelation 3:6, but also included in the Revelation passage was a reference to the seven horns. So we have these images to consider.

1. The Seven Spirits: Seven is God's number of perfection. The Scriptures said that Jesus had these seven spirits. This concept of perfection or fullness agrees with John 3:34 (NKJV): "For He whom God has sent speaks the words of God, for God does not give the Spirit by measure." Therefore, Jesus had the fullness of the Spirit without limitations, which produced God's perfection.

2. The Seven Eyes: These seven eyes represent spiritual vision. Jesus had 20/20 spiritual vision. These eyes represent the ability to see by the Spirit into the Spirit world.

3. The Seven Horns: Prophetically, horns represent spiritual authority and power. Jesus has been given all authority in heaven and on earth (Matthew 28:18). Again, the number seven indicates complete authority.

4. The Seven Lamps of Fire: These represent the baptism of the Holy Spirit. John the Baptist said that Jesus would baptize with the Holy Spirit and fire. Zechariah wrote that the temple would be built "not by might nor by power (of men), but by My Spirit, says the Lord of Hosts." It then stands to reason that the latter temple, the New Testament church, would be built by the Holy Spirit. The purifying fire of the Spirit will be demonstrated through those who are baptized by the Holy Spirit.

Jesus was baptized in the Jordan when the Holy Spirit came upon him in the form of a dove (Matthew 3:16). He told his disciples to wait for the promise of the Father before they left Jerusalem (Acts 1:4), and he said in Acts 1:8 NKJV "But you shall receive power when the Holy Spirit has come upon you; and you shall be witnesses to Me in Jerusalem, and in all Judea and Samaria, and to the end of the earth."

Let us define these seven spirits of God that reign and rule in the kingdom of God. Don't get restless! You may have to put this book down and pray for revelation from God. So then faith comes by hearing and hearing by the word of God." (Romans 10:17 NKJV)

In Isaiah, we find the definition of these seven spirits of God that Jesus possessed and that were Lord of the kingdom of God, the one who has power and authority over others, in this case, the seven spirits.

> And the spirit of the Lord shall rest upon him, the spirit of wisdom and understanding, the spirit of counsel and might, the spirit of knowledge and of the fear of the Lord; And shall make him of quick understanding in the fear of the Lord: and he shall not judge after the sight of his eyes, neither reprove after the hearing of his ears. (Isaiah 11:2:3 KJV)

The reign and rule of the kingdom of God is at the seat of authority there. When we submit to the authority of the throne of God to reign and rule over our lives, something mysterious, supernatural, comes into play. We are no longer mere mortals; we become mighty in God and can pull down the strongholds of our minds. We take on God's nature and mind. We say, "Let this mind that was also in Christ Jesus be our mind." We take on God's powerful attributes. This is why Jesus was able to do what he did, and this is why we will also be able to do what he did.

Moses was able to part the Red Sea because he didn't rely on his ability or insight but used the seven spirits of God. The kingdom of God came on the scene and altered time and space to allow the children of Israel free passage to dry land. Before you say, "That was Jesus! We're talking about Moses," let me give you one more Scripture that will prove your ability to do what God said you could do.

> Beware lest anyone cheat you through philosophy and empty deceit, according to the tradition of men, according to the basic principles of the world, and not according to Christ. For in Him dwells all the

fullness of the Godhead bodily; and you are complete
in Him, who is the head of all principality and power.
(Colossians 2:8–10 NKJV)

Stop saying it was meant for someone else! Don't be cheated
out of your inheritance in the kingdom of God through philosophy
and empty deceit that relies on the tradition of men. In the
kingdom of God, you aren't operating under the basic principles
of this world but under the auspices of Christ, the anointed one.
The Word of God says you're complete in Jesus Christ, the head
of all principalities and powers. Let the kingdom of God reign
and rule in your life today. The seven spirits of God are wisdom,
understanding, counsel, might, knowledge, fear of the Lord, and
quick understanding.

In the next chapter, we will discuss who the King of the kingdom
of God is.

Chapter 2

Introduction to the King

In many conversations I've been in, many people couldn't tell me the meaning of the word *Christ*. Even today, many believe it was Jesus' last name. According to the *Holman Bible Dictionary*, *Christ* means "anointed one"; it comes from the Greek *christos*, "anointed." *Messiah* in Hebrew is *mashiach*, again, the "anointed one."[3] Christ is the messianic authority of Jesus.

Prophecy of the Messiah Jesus Christ

Hundreds of years before the birth of Jesus, the prophet Isaiah foretold the reign and rule of the Jesus the Messiah, the Christ. Isaiah 9:6–7 tells us,

> Unto us a Child is born, unto us a Son is given, and the government will be upon His shoulder. So His name will be called Wonderful, Counselor, Mighty God, Everlasting Father, and Prince of Peace. Of the increase of His government and peace there will be no end, upon the throne of David and over His

---

[3] Holman Illustrated Bible Dictionary (Holman Reference; Revised edition (October 1, 2003)

kingdom, to order it and establish it with judgment
and justice from that time forward, even forever.
The zeal of the Lord of hosts will perform this.

This prophecy was fulfilled in Jesus Christ, as we will see later.

The child born to the Virgin Mary was Jesus of Nazareth, the
Son of God. Jesus identified God as his Father in Matthew 8:29: "And
suddenly they cried out, saying, 'What have we to do with You,
Jesus, You Son of God? Have you come here to torment us before
the time?'" In Matthew 16:16, we read, "Simon Peter answered and
said, 'You are the Christ, the Son of the living God.'"

Something alarming in Isaiah 9:7 verifies Jesus Christ as the
King of God's kingdom. The statement "Of the increase of His
government and peace there will be no end, upon the throne
of David and over His kingdom, to order it and establish it with
judgment and justice from that time forward, even forever" sticks
out like a sore thumb. It means a real kingdom of eternal peace
is coming. Jesus, the Messiah, will sit on David's throne and rule
his kingdom. He will establish his kingdom and arrange it to suit
his divine purposes. The charts below further outlines prophesy
concerning this.

Prophecy	Fulfillment
Zechariah 3:8 "Hear now, O Joshua the high priest, thou, and thy fellows that sit before thee: for they are men wondered at: for, behold, I will bring forth my servant the BRANCH."	**John 17:4** "I have glorified thee on the earth: I have finished the work which thou gavest me to do."

Zechariah 6:12–13	Hebrews 8:1
"And <u>speak</u> unto him, saying, Thus speaketh the Lord of hosts, saying, Behold the man whose name is The BRANCH; and he shall grow up out of his place, and he shall build the temple of the Lord: Even he shall build the temple of the Lord; and he shall bear the glory, and shall sit and rule upon his throne; and he shall be a priest upon his throne: and the counsel of peace shall be between them both."	"NOW of the things which we have spoken this is the sum: We have such an high priest, who is set on the right hand of the throne of the Majesty in the heavens;" **Romans 8:34** "Who is he that condemneth? It is Christ that died, yea rather, that is risen again, who is even at the right hand of God, who also maketh intercession for us."
Zechariah 9:9 "Rejoice greatly, O daughter of Zion; shout, O daughter of Jerusalem: behold, thy King cometh unto thee: he is just, and having salvation; lowly, and riding upon an ass, and upon a colt the foal of an ass."	**Matthew 21:8–10** "And a very great multitude spread their garments in the way; others cut down branches from the trees, and strawed them in the way. And the multitudes that went before, and that followed, cried, saying, Hosanna to the son of David: Blessed is he that cometh in the name of the Lord; Hosanna in the highest. And when he was come into Jerusalem, all the city was moved, saying, Who is this?"

Jesus Christ, the Son of God, sits at the right hand of his Father forever making intercession for us who believe (Mark 16:19; Hebrews 12:2). He was the Word made flesh who dwelt among us. There is no other name more popular in the world today than the name of Jesus Christ. The Word of God teaches us there is salvation in no one else, for there is no other name under heaven given to us by which we can be saved.

The name of Jesus Christ has stood the test of time. God has highly exalted him and bestowed on him the name that is above every other so that at the name of Jesus, every knee should bow in heaven and on earth and under earth, and every tongue should confess that Jesus Christ is Lord, to the glory of God the Father.

We were washed, sanctified, and justified in the name of the Lord Jesus Christ and by the Spirit of our God. In a latter chapter, we will discuss justification and righteousness, but in short, "justified" means we're no longer guilty due to our sins; it's as if we'd never sinned. Through further examination of the life and history of Jesus, we will learn he is the way, the truth, and the life, and no one can come to the Father except through Jesus Christ. Finally, after carefully researching the book of Revelation, we find these passages of scripture And out of his mouth goeth a sharp sword, that with it he should smite the nations: and he shall rule them with a rod of iron: and he treadeth the winepress of the fierceness and wrath of Almighty God.

[16] And he hath on his vesture and on his thigh a name written, KING OF KINGS, AND LORD OF LORDS. (Revelation 19:15-16 KJV) This same Jesus is declared to be King of Kings and Lord of Lords. Jesus Christ is the Son of God and the undisputed King reigning and ruling over all kings and kingdoms. I believe with all my heart that there is a kingdom coming soon that will rule our hearts and will be a physical kingdom on earth. Striking down the nations and ruling them with a rod of iron sounds more physical than only spiritual to me.

This is why the kingdom of God is the foundation and central theme of Jesus' teaching. Everywhere Jesus went, he made it a big point to teach the people about the kingdom of God. Why has his message become obsolete? What has broken the line of communication we used to have to Jesus?

Chinese Whispers

Chinese whispers is a game played around the world. It's called "telephone" in the United States; one person whispers a message to another, who whispers it to yet another, down through a line of people until the last player announces the message he or she heard to the group. Most of the time, errors accumulate in the retellings and the statement announced by the last player differs significantly and often amusingly from the one uttered by the first. The reasons for the changes in the message include anxiety, impatience, erroneous corrections, and deliberate alteration.

I'll use Matthew 13:24–25 to explain this. A farmer once planted wheat. When the wheat started growing, another plant, "tare," began to grow with it. The tare that Jesus described in this parable was also known as the darnel seed, which looks almost exactly like wheat in the beginning stages of its growth. However, after it grows a little more, it becomes evident that it is a weed, and it actually uproots the wheat.

In time, the farmer learned that tare was growing with his wheat. Jesus explained how the Enemy had come when everyone was asleep and had mixed tare seed in with the wheat. The farmer, who hadn't known this, had sown both seeds. This is the way it is now in the world. Jesus preached the gospel of the kingdom of God, but through the years, his enemies have crept in unawares and distorted the gospel of the kingdom of God.

These satanic plants have undermined the Word of God; they have deliberately distorted the message of Jesus and used subtle changes to change how the gospel of the kingdom is heard and understood.

Jesus gave the disciples the breakdown of his parable of the sower in (Mark 4:15 KJV) "And these are they by the way side, where the word is sown; but when they have heard, Satan cometh immediately, and taketh away the word that was sown in their hearts." When the gospel of the kingdom of God is preached or taught, the Enemy will come immediately to take away the Word or distort it to prevent it from taking root in a person's heart. Just as in the game of Chinese whispers, demons will alter the message.

A real kingdom is coming to supplant all the kingdoms in the world today.

Chapter 3

The Kingdom Rules in Our Hearts

The heart is our central intelligence facility; everything comes out of it. It's the seat of affection; it's where the soul resides. Our mouths speak out of the abundance of our hearts and proclaim whatever is in our hearts. King Solomon stated the matter of the heart very eloquently: "Keep thy heart with all diligence, for out of it are the out flowings of life" (Proverbs 4:23 NKJV).

After he had compromised his position with God by committing adultery with Bathsheba, King David cried out to God to create in him a clean heart and renew his spirit. The heart is one of our most sophisticated organs; all our life functions rely on it. The Bible has much to say about the heart. The word *heart* appears 835 times in 775 verses in the NKJV. The study of the heart is thus a massive and complex undertaking. God knows all our hearts: "For you alone know the hearts of all the sons of men" (1 Kings 8:39 NKJV).

When the Bible speaks of the human heart, it's speaking of our thinking, our will, our emotions and feelings, our conscience, and any combinations of these. However, the word may also refer to our whole inner being. Each of these aspects of the heart is worth taking a look at.

The heart is our thinking aspect. "For as he thinks in his heart, so is he" (Proverbs 23:7 NKJV). Jesus asked, "Why do you think evil in your hearts?" (Matthew 9:4 NKJV). "For out of the heart proceed evil thoughts" (Matthew 15:19 NKJV). "If that evil servant says in his heart, 'My master is delaying his coming ...'" (Matthew 24:48 NKJV). The evil servant said this in his heart because that is what he was thinking. "But Mary kept all these things and pondered them in her heart" (Luke 2:19 NKJV). Mary thought over these things in her mind. One could find many more verses that teach the same thing about the heart being the place of thought, reasoning, and understanding.

We Are Sanctified in Our Hearts

People have turned the doctrine of sanctification into a religious system though it was designed simply to allow the kingdom of God to effectively rule our hearts. *To sanctify* means to set apart for a sacred purpose, to make holy.

The heart is where the kingdom of God sets up residence, and we will discuss this later. The heart is to be a sacred place. Jesus enters our hearts as an invited guest, but more than that, as our King and Lord. If we refuse to allow him to sit on the throne of our heart, he will not consent to be our guest. Many try to limit him to being their weekend guest at church, sort of like a part-time lover or visitor you have over for dinner. Come Monday, he is expected to leave until another time of fellowship.

It cannot be this way! The Scripture reference for this is in 1 Peter: "Sanctify Christ as Lord in your hearts, always being ready to make a defense to everyone that asks you to give an account for the hope that is in you, yet with gentleness and reverence."

The Kingdom Rules the Spiritual Realm

Because the kingdom of God is the rule of God, wherever the Lord Jesus Christ reigns is the kingdom of God; this applies to the individual and the multitudes. God isn't a physical being even though he will affect the physical. God is a Spirit (John 4:24), and his kingdom is in the spiritual realm, invisible to our natural eyes. Someday, God's kingdom will come in all its fullness and reveal itself in the physical sense; however, it's now "at hand" for us to enter by faith. God writes the laws of his kingdom on our hearts (Jeremiah 31:33–34) and calls us to walk in obedience to his commands. Through the guidance and power of the Holy Spirit, we can experience the reign of God in our daily lives. When we yield to God's authority in obedience to his Word, we submit to kingdom rule in our life.

The Spirit of God reveals the ways of God to the children of God. In 1 Corinthians 2:9–10 we read,

> But as it is written, Eye hath not seen, nor ear heard, neither have entered into the heart of man, the things which God hath prepared for them that love him. But God hath revealed them unto us by his Spirit: for the Spirit searches all things, even, the deep things of God.

The rule and reign of God in our hearts is the reality of the kingdom of God on earth!

Chapter 4

The Kingdom of God and the Church

The relationship between the church and the kingdom of God is often misunderstood. Christians often speak as if the kingdom of God was just another name for the church. In fact, they differ, and the kingdom of God is much more important. Jesus came to establish the kingdom of God; this is clear from the basic message he proclaimed: "The time has come. The kingdom of God is near. Repent and believe the good news" (Mark 1:15).

The church is an assembly of believers. The church is also known as *ecclesia*. Jesus told Peter in Matthew 16:18, "Upon this rock I will build my church." Jesus didn't say "Upon this rock I will build my kingdom." Matthew, Mark, Luke, and John tell us that Jesus was constantly teaching about the kingdom of God. The good news he proclaimed was the gospel of the kingdom, the government, of God. The twelve disciples were sent out to proclaim the same gospel of the kingdom (Luke 9:1–2). In contrast, the gospels mention the word *church* only twice.

The kingdom of God is a much wider concept than the church is. The kingdom includes every area of life under the rule and authority of God; whatever God rules is part of the kingdom. Businesses run on biblical principles are part of the kingdom. All human activity done according to his will is part of the kingdom of God. God wants his kingdom to expand into every area of life. This expansion takes place in two ways. First, people must be born into the kingdom. Jesus said that unless we are born of water and the Spirit, we cannot enter the kingdom of God (John 3:5). When people are born again through repentance and faith in Jesus Christ, they became citizens of the kingdom. God will deliver them from sickness and the power of the Devil. Being born again is the only way a person can enter the kingdom of God.

The second way the kingdom expands is when Christians bring the different aspects of their lives under the will of God. As Christians apply the principles of God's Word to those activities over which he has authority, they became part of the kingdom of God. The government of God expands as Christians extend the rule of God into the areas of life where they have authority. Authority is an essential aspect of any kingdom.

The government of God becomes reality when every sphere of authority is ruled according to the Word of God. This happens when those with authority are Christians who submit to God's authority. He has delegated authority to individuals and groups. When a sphere of delegated authority is ruled according to his will, it becomes part of his kingdom. Where authority is exercised contrary to his will, that sphere of authority is outside the kingdom.

At the same time, the interaction between the various spheres of authority must also be governed by the Word of God. It's wrong for one group to take over the authority that belongs to another. For example, when the civil government becomes the provider, it's taking over authority and responsibility God has assigned to the family. Each delegated authority must carry out only the functions God has assigned to it.

Everything outside the kingdom of God is part of the kingdom of darkness ruled and controlled by Satan. His kingdom is characterized by disunity and conflict, which are the consequences of human sin. Satan is a liar and destroyer, so his kingdom will be full of hatred, bitterness, and destruction of human life. The only way to escape is through faith in Jesus Christ (Colossians 1:13). Naturally, the two kingdoms will engage in warfare. God's purpose is to extend his kingdom throughout the world, while Satan is trying to expand his kingdom as well. Christians who have withdrawn from many spheres of authority make his task easier. The idea has developed that politics and business are improper activities for Christians, so these two very important areas of authority have been handed over to the Devil. Even when Christians are involved in politics and business, there has been no serious attempt to apply biblical principles to these activities. This has severely weakened the government of God.

Instead of seeking to establish the kingdom of God, Christians have concentrated on building the church. The church has become a place of retreat from the world. It may have supported Christians in their daily lives, but to the world, it appears weak, irrelevant. Rather than being a place of retreat, the church should be a recruiting station and training ground for members of the kingdom of God.

It must recruit members for the kingdom by proclaiming the gospel. At the same time, it must send Christians out into the world to establish the kingdom of God. Christians should move into every area of authority and take up responsibility there. The church should teach these Christians to exercise that authority in accordance with the Word of God.

Jesus talked about the kingdom of God incessantly (Mark 1:14–15; Luke 4:23; John 3:3), but he mentioned the church only twice. Jesus preached the good news of the kingdom, but the modern church tends to preach the gospel of personal salvation or the gospel of the church; the gospel of the kingdom is rarely heard, and the gospel of the government of God is never heard. The reason is that most Christians think the kingdom of God is just another name for the church, but it's a much broader concept than the church in that what it preaches is much broader than the gospel of personal salvation. If we are to obey Jesus and proclaim the gospel of the kingdom of God, we must recover a vision of the kingdom of God.

The church is just one sphere of authority within the kingdom of God. For too long, too many has seen it as the only one. The church must never be an end in itself; it must always be working to establish the kingdom of God. When Jesus comes back, he doesn't want to find just a holy church. He's coming back for a victorious church, a church that has established the kingdom of God as a reality in the world.

Chapter 5

Where Is the Kingdom of God?

Now when He was asked by the Pharisees when the kingdom of
God would come, He answered them and said, "The kingdom of
God does not come with observation; nor will they say, 'See here!'
or 'See there!' For indeed, the kingdom of God is within you."
—Luke 17:20–21 NKJV

Where is the kingdom of God? That's an age-old question; the
disciples asked Jesus this in anticipation of the restoring of the
kingdom to Israel. This was after he had risen from the dead and
returned to give commandments to his apostles. They had walked
with Jesus and seen his actions daily; they had witnessed Jesus
perform many miracles. They were commanded not to depart from
Jerusalem but wait for the promise of the Father. He told them how
John had baptized with water but they would be baptized with the
Holy Spirit. However, because they finally realized he was truly
the Son of God, they asked, "Lord, will you restore at this time the
Kingdom to Israel?" (Acts 1:6 NKJV) I am sure the response they
got wasn't what they had looked forward to especially seeing he
had all power in his hand.

Jesus answered, "It is not for you to know the times or the seasons, which the Father has placed in his own authority." Jesus was setting the apostles up for something even greater than the physical restoration of the kingdom to Israel. When Jesus told them they would receive power after the Holy Spirit came upon them, he was basically conferring on them and us his supernatural authority.

Science Fiction—A Glimpse of the Future

I was intrigued by science fiction when I was a kid. Programs such as *Lost in Space* and *Star Trek* were my favorites. Some of what we saw on those shows has become reality. I thought warp drive was only on *Star Trek*, but recently, I read an article with a startling title: "Warp Drive May be more feasible than thought, Scientists Say."[4] Imagine a spaceship traveling faster than light! The reason I brought this up is that all things are possible in the kingdom of God. The idea of something as large as a kingdom being housed internally is not unrealistic at all. A few years ago, I watched the movie *Men in Black*.[5] Even though it was fiction, it made a lot of sense to me. In the movie was a cat named Orion,[6] who belonged to the character Gentle Rosenburg, an Arquilian on earth who was a member of the Arquilian royal family. Rosenburg was always seen with his cat, whom he treated like royalty. Despite appearing to have a small role in the film, Orion had a large role in it.

After Rosenburg was killed by Edgar the Bug, Orion was left at the morgue. When Jay and Kay (the "Men in Black") investigated, Jay accidentally discovered the Arquilian in disguise, who revealed that

---

[4] Claudia Moskowitz, "Warp Drive May Be More Feasible Than Thought, Scientists Say"; Space.com, September 17, 2012.
[5] *Men in Black* was a 1997 film directed by Barry Sonnenfeld and starring Tommy Lee Jones and Will Smith.
[6] "Men in Black"; meninblack.wikia.com/wiki/Orion.

the Arquilian Galaxy, which Edgar the Bug was looking for, was on Orion's belt, which the men in black took to mean the trio of stars in space. However, after talking with Frank the Pug, they realized that a galaxy could be as small as a marble but still contain billions of stars.

I guess by now you're thinking, *What's his point? Science fiction? Warp travel? Now Orion the cat?* But attached to Orion's "belt," his collar, was an ornament that housed a galaxy containing billions of stars. If science fiction can do all this with a galaxy in an ornament hanging from a cat's neck, it's not that far-fetched to think of an entire kingdom residing in a person's heart.

With this sidebar concluded, let's dissect this passage of Scripture.

Breaking Down the Scripture

When the Pharisees asked Jesus when the kingdom of God would come, Jesus said the kingdom didn't come though observation; no one could see the kingdom of God at that time, only in the future. (More about this later.) As did most believers, the Pharisees believed what they could actually see. The whole unseen, spiritual world out there operates simultaneously with the physical world. Faith is not based on what we can see but on what we believe and have knowledge of. Faith is the substance of things that we hope for and the evidence of things not seen. My definition reads something like this: confident belief in an idea or thing has mass and occupies space, giving substance to it and making it real or actual. It becomes an outward sign of an entity existing in space and time though not yet perceived with the eyes.

Jesus intended to teach the Pharisees that the things they could see were temporary while the things they couldn't see were eternal (2 Corinthians 4:18). So the kingdom of God is not visible to the naked eye. The next thing Jesus said was that the kingdom of God was not here or there. I hear preachers saying all the time, "The kingdom is here!" When Jesus told the Pharisees, "The kingdom of God is within you," they probably looked at each other perplexed, but Jesus didn't have a hidden agenda. Many have taught that what Jesus said had only one aspect, but I believe it had two.

In the previous chapter, we discussed the kingdom of God ruling in our hearts and determined that God's kingdom would reign in the heart. Jesus was giving the Pharisees an understanding way deeper than what they imagined. Let's look at Jesus' words. The word *within* in Greek is *entos*, "in the midst of." Praise God! Jesus was not only saying he ruled and reigned in hearts; he was also saying, "Oh by the way, Pharisees, the kingdom of God is in the midst of you right now because I brought it with me." Wherever Jesus is, the kingdom of God is all around him. The United States has ambassadors and embassies in other countries, so wherever that embassy is, the United States is right there as well. Likewise, wherever and whenever Jesus shows up, the kingdom of God shows up and is right there, internally or in our midst.

God's kingdom literally exists and is alive; it reigns and rules our daily lives. Before we get into the biblical prophecies concerning the kingdom of God, I want you to know it is written "the just shall live by faith" in several passages of Scripture.

- "Now the just shall live by faith: but if any man draw back, my soul shall have no pleasure in him" (Hebrews 10:38).
- "For in it the righteousness of God is revealed from faith for faith, as it is written, 'The righteous shall live by faith'" (Romans 1:17).
- "Behold, his soul which is lifted up is not upright in him: but the just shall live by his faith" (Habakkuk 2:4).

My friend, you'll have to catch this "kingdom of God" teaching based on faith. You'll have to release your faith in God's Word. Believe it. Stand on it. Don't rely on what I've written in the book; search out the Scriptures, meditate on them, and start practicing what they say. The kingdom of God is a real kingdom ready to come and rule in your life.

Chapter 6

Daniel and the Kingdom

The name Daniel means "God is my Judge" (Ezekiel 14:14, 20). The book of Daniel is one of the most important books of the Bible. Daniel was a minor prophet with a major message; he bridged the Old and New Testaments. The book of Daniel parallels the book of Revelation. Through Daniel, God revealed the exact day, month, and year of the Messiah's death and events leading to his return.

The book of Daniel demonstrates God's comprehension of and complete control over time and nations by giving detailed prophecies about the succession of kingdoms and rulers. Daniel foretells the eventual establishment of the Messiah's kingdom, which will overthrow the kingdoms of this world. Over 2,500 years ago, God gave Daniel, a Jewish prophet, special understanding of future world governments. While Daniel was serving in the court of Nebuchadnezzar, the king of Babylon, God revealed to Daniel details about the kingdom of God becoming the final rule and authority in the world.

> And in the days of these kings shall the God of heaven set up a kingdom, which shall never be destroyed: and the kingdom shall not be left to other people, but it shall break in pieces and consume all

these kingdoms, and it shall stand for ever. (Daniel 2:44 KJV)

These prophetic words revealed the central theme of Jesus Christ's message while he was on earth. Daniel had just concluded giving the interpretation of a dream the king had had. This dream dealt with kingdoms that would come after Babylon. Daniel revealed that during the time of these kingdoms, God would eventually reestablish his kingdom on earth as it was during the time of Adam and Eve. They had experienced kingdom rule before being exiled from the garden of Eden. Daniel wrote that when God set up this kingdom, which would never be destroyed, it would not be left to other people but would break up all the kingdoms of earth permanently: "But the saints of the most High shall take the kingdom, and possess the kingdom for ever, even for ever and ever" (Daniel 7:18 KJV).

Daniel's prophecy explained that the saints of the most high God (those who have accepted Jesus Christ as Lord and Savior) would possess the kingdom of God. Jesus had told Nicodemus that he had to be born again to enter the kingdom of God.

> I saw in the night visions, and, behold, one like the Son of man came with the clouds of heaven, and came to the Ancient of days, and they brought him near before him. And there was given him dominion, and glory, and a kingdom, that all people, nations, and languages, should serve him: his dominion is an everlasting dominion, which shall not pass away, and his kingdom that which shall not be destroyed. (Daniel 7:13–14)

The kingdom of God will be set up on earth (I'll explain this later) after the rapture of the believers. Daniel had a vision of the Son of man coming from the clouds. Look at the similarities in 1 Thessalonians.

> We are telling you what the Lord taught. We who are still alive when the Lord comes will not go into his kingdom ahead of those who have already died. The Lord will come from heaven with a command, with the voice of the archangel, and with the trumpet call of God. First, the dead who believed in Christ will come back to life. Then, together with them, we who are still alive will be taken in the clouds to meet the Lord in the air. In this way we will always be with the Lord. (1 Thessalonians 4:15–17 GWT)

And look at what Revelation proclaims.

> Behold, he cometh with clouds; and every eye shall see him, and they also which pierced him: and all kindreds of the earth shall wail because of him. Even so, Amen. I am Alpha and Omega, the beginning and the ending, saith the Lord, which is, and which was, and which is to come, the Almighty. (Revelation 1:7–8)

This is awesome! Daniel predicted these events!

Here's where it really gets good. God was going to give his Son dominion, glory, and a kingdom; all people, nations, and languages would serve the King of Kings. He would have eternal dominion. Kings always have dominion, glory, and kingdoms.

It gets better. Look at this: "Until the Ancient of days came, and judgment was given to the saints of the most High; and the time came that the saints possessed the kingdom" (Daniel 7:22 KJV). The saints or the believers will judge in this kingdom as well as possess it.

> And the kingdom and dominion, and the greatness of the kingdom under the whole heaven, shall be given to the people of the saints of the most high, whose kingdom is an everlasting kingdom, and all dominions shall serve and obey him. (Daniel 7:27 KJV)

This is so powerful! The greatness of the kingdom of God shall be released to the people who are the saints of the Most High. The kingdom of God is everlasting, and everyone everywhere will serve and obey the King of Kings, the Lord of Lords.

From Daniel's prophetic word, we can see that the kingdom of God will be set up on earth. After it's established, all earthly kingdoms will come to an end. This prophesied kingdom will not simply be a philosophical movement limited to human thought or reside in human hearts. It will not be an invisible kingdom. It will be an actual kingdom with territory, a ruler, laws, and subjects (the saints of the most high God), and it will rule over all the nations on earth.

When Jesus came to earth, the world's ruling empires prophesied by Daniel hadn't run their course. It was not time for God's kingdom to replace all human governments on earth. On trial before Pilate, Jesus said, "My kingdom is not of this world. If My kingdom were of this world, my servants would fight, so that I should not be handed over to my accusers; but now my kingdom is not from here" (John

18:36). But the fact that the kingdom of God hadn't yet come to earth didn't stop the disciples from asking questions about this most important subject. After all, Jesus had taught them to pray for this kingdom to come and to make it the first priority in their lives (Matthew 6:10, 33).

The Importance of This Message

In spite of all the killings, disappointments, world problems, hunger, and human trafficking, a real kingdom is coming. The kingdom of God shall supersede all other kingdoms of the world. The United States, Great Britain, Russia, China, and the rest of the world powers will bow to this new kingdom Jesus talked about. Romans 14:11 KJV tells us, "For it is written, As I live, saith the Lord, every knee shall bow to me, and every tongue shall confess to God." Why else would God have shown Daniel and several other prophets these events? Why would Jesus have proclaimed the gospel of the kingdom of God? He preached the gospel of the kingdom of God: "The time is fulfilled, and the kingdom of God is at hand. Repent, and believe in the gospel" (Mark 1:14–15).

When Jesus said the kingdom of God was "at hand," he meant his authority as the King was available right then. The instructions he ultimately gave to the people needing to enter the kingdom were then available to all who understood his message about repenting of sin and believing in the gospel. This was only a small number of people, as recording in Acts; only 120 had assembled in the upper room on the day of Pentecost.

Won't you repent of your sins today? Bow your head and pray this prayer to God with me: "Lord Jesus, I confess all my sins to you, those that I know about and those that are hidden. Lord Jesus, I surrender my life to you at this moment. I repent of all my sins.

I denounce sin in my life. I turn away from sin and toward you in righteousness. Lord Jesus, I open the door of my heart and ask you to come in. Let your kingdom come into my life from this day forward. I believe that you are Lord and Christ, amen."

Chapter 7

How to Seek the Kingdom of God

But seek ye first the kingdom of God, and his righteousness;
and all these things shall be added unto you.
—Matthew 6:33

Most all electronics come with owners' manuals, and knock-down furniture comes with assembly instructions. I love to cook and enjoy watching people eat in silence because the age-old recipes my mother had had handed down to her are so tasty.

Likewise, we have to follow certain procedures to inherit well-being. Jesus put it like this: whatever you want in your life, put it in someone else's life. Paul explained it by writing, "Be not deceived, God is not mocked: for whatsoever a man soweth, that shall he also reap." (Galatians 6:9 KJV) The seeds you plant in life will produce a harvest sooner than you think. Jesus gave us a recipe to utilize the kingdom of God's power, a pathway to success in life. This is kingdom talk at its finest. If you can follow what's being said here and embrace its hidden truth, the things you desire shall be added graciously to you.

We're instructed to seek something, to gravitate toward it, to find it by any means necessary. Seeking something requires that we look for it. We'll discover something when we start seeking it. I always allude to the words of Jesus Christ because he is my King. Jesus said that if we seek, we will find (Matthew 7:7). Students have spent many a day and night trying to attain the hidden knowledge that comes through study. George Patton said, "Prepare for the unknown by studying how others in the past have coped with the unforeseeable and the unpredictable."[7]

What Am I Seeking?

If you seek the kingdom of God, you'll have to seek God's way of doing things; you'll have to learn God's system by studying his Word: "Study to shew thyself approved unto God, a workman that needeth not to be ashamed, rightly dividing the word of truth" (2 Timothy 2:15).

God gave Joshua important instructions after he assumed leadership of the children of Israel. He told Joshua that if he wanted success, he'd have to understand his system and way of doing things. God told Joshua not to let the book of the Law, his Word, depart his mouth but to meditate day and night; then he would achieve success and would prosper (Joshua 1:8).

Meditation is more than simply thinking; it's also saying. Saying and thinking the Word will engrave it in your heart, the place the kingdom of God reigns and rules. King David put it like this: "My heart was hot within me, while I was musing the fire burned: then spake I with my tongue" (Psalm 39:3). As King David mused, as he thought deeply, something happened. His heart was hot because the kingdom of God had taken control. Once that happened, King

---

[7] George Smith Patton, Jr. (1885–1945), was a general in the U.S. Army best known for his command of the Seventh and Third Armies; Wikipedia

David started to speak and say what God had said, and that meant he was destined to have what he said.

Something supernatural happens when we start decreeing what God says. Isaiah 55:11 (KJV) tells us, "So shall my word be that goeth forth out of my mouth: it shall not return unto me void, but it shall accomplish that which I please, and it shall prosper in the thing whereto I sent it." When we speak the Word, it won't return empty. The Word will accomplish everything it was meant to accomplish and make it prosper. Praise God!

Angels Get Involved

When you seek the kingdom of God, angels will become involved in your quest. Angels are God's ministering spirits sent to minister for the heirs of salvation, the heirs of the kingdom of God. Imagine being ministered to by a waiter at a restaurant; angels do the same thing. When they hear the Word of God, they carry it out. Consider this: "The Lord hath prepared his throne in the heavens; and his kingdom ruleth over all. Bless the Lord, ye his angels, that excel in strength, that do his commandments, hearkening unto the voice of his word" (Psalm 10:19–20).

God's throne is in the heavens, his seat of authority, from which he rules everything. When the angels hear the Word of God coming from your mouth, they excel in strength and carry out the assignment in the Word of God. God has way of releasing exactly what we asked for, when praying in agreement with his word, to the heirs of the kingdom—you and me. It's not some pie-in-the-sky system or a system of hoping and praying; it's a system of divine release.

My Encounter

I write here about my encounter with God's angels; I call it my "flapping my wings" experience. I went through years of alcoholism and absolute sinfulness. I would leave church after preaching and my wife wouldn't see me for days at a time. One day after a serious binge, I lay on my bed and cried out to God for deliverance. I said, "Father, I'm tired of this condition, and it's written that anyone who calls on the Lord will be delivered" (Joel 2:32). I heard loud clapping in my ear; it was so powerful that I broke out in sweat. It went on for a while. I felt something touching my face. After the noise and the touching, I never had problems with alcoholism; I've been delivered for years now.

Later on, I found out through research and prayer that angels excel in strength as they listen to the voice of God's Word. What I'd heard was angels getting busy with their assignment—carrying out God's Word. Praise God! I don't care what your situation is; when you use God's Word, something will happen for your good. I'm living testimony of what God can do.

Seek what God has said and promised in his Word. Meditate on it. Let the fire start burning, be bold, and declare what God has said. Put it out there, man! Call those things that are not as though they were. Put yourself in the state of it already having happened. Feel it, know it, stand on it. Job said that if you decree a thing, it will be established unto you and the light will shine upon your ways. Look at this same verse in the Amplified Bible: "You shall also decide *and* decree a thing, and it shall be established for you; and the light [of God's favor] shall shine upon your ways" (Job 22:28). Powerful words.

I have made God's system a priority in my life. I understand this system and use it like clockwork. God's system involves studying, understanding, and using his Word; it means declaring what he has said and has promised. God's system should always take priority over everything else in your life. Jesus said, "With man things are impossible, but with God all things are possible" All things are governed and control by the Word of God, which was there in the beginning; the Word was and still is God. All things were made by his Word, and without it, nothing was made.

You have the secret power of creation in your knowledge and your tongue. Death and life are in the power of the tongue. All things are upheld by the Word, his power. Jesus told us to seek the kingdom of God, to understand God's way of doing things in all matters. This requires discovering God's wisdom in all matters in life in his Word. "God's word is a lamp unto my feet, and a light unto my path" (Psalm 119:105). When you use the Word of God for guidance, it will become the guiding lamp for your feet and your faith, the means by which you will walk in his path. Life can at times seem dark as the desert at midnight, but the wisdom of the Word will illuminate your path and make it as clear as day.

I spent the majority of this chapter just seeking the kingdom of God; let me now discuss his righteousness.

Chapter 8

His Righteousness

For I say unto you, that except your righteousness shall
exceed the righteousness of the scribes and Pharisees,
ye shall in no case enter into the kingdom of heaven.
Matthew 5:20 KJV

We tend to focus on one aspect of Scripture and miss the mark because we neglect one very important point. Jesus said, "Seek ye first the Kingdom of God," but most people leave out a key word. Many of us have heard that if we just seek God's kingdom, we can have whatever we need or want. This is true, but we leave out the part that reads, "All these things will be added unto you." When we discount what God is saying because of our tendency to change words around to justify our positions, we have a serious problem. The meat in this sandwich is righteousness.

Righteousness means having right standing with God, not humanity. So often we attempt to please others and satisfy their needs. Most leaders would much rather please others than please God. Seeking God's kingdom walks hand in hand with righteousness. The very first stage of righteousness, the very core of its understanding, is simple but often neglected.

Jesus stated this philosophy during one of his many debates with the Pharisees and Sadducees, who were always trying to disqualify what Jesus was saying. They asked Jesus questions to catch him in a lie or make people doubt what he was saying. During one of these moments, Jesus said,

> and thou shalt love the Lord thy God with all thy heart, and with all thy soul, and with all thy mind, and with all thy strength: this is the first commandment. And the second is like, namely this, Thou shalt love thy neighbour as thyself. There is none other commandment greater than these. (Matthew 22:37 KJV)

We must adapt our lives and relationships to these words. Being righteous means loving God with all our heart. In previous chapters, we discussed the importance of clean hearts worthy of God dwelling in them. We must love God with our complete hearts. The interchange of the heart and the mind is not complex; our hearts are our minds, our actual beings. Jesus told us to love God with all our minds and being. Scripture, mainly in the Law of Moses, states this concept: "You shall love the Lord your God with all your heart, with all your soul, and with all your strength" (Deuteronomy 6:5).

We must love God with our souls, which have often been misrepresented as our spirits. To shed light on this soul business, I'll quote Watchman Nee's *Spiritual Man.*[8]

---

[8] Watchman Nee (倪柝声, Ni To-sheng, 1903–1972) was a church leader and Christian teacher who worked in China during the first half of the twentieth century.

Spirit, Soul, and Body—Watchman Nee

Watchman Nee wrote,

> The ordinary concept of the constitution of human beings is dualistic-soul and body. According to this concept soul is the invisible inner spiritual part, while body is the visible outer corporal part. Though there is some truth to this, it is nevertheless inaccurate. Such an opinion comes from fallen man, not from God; apart from God's revelation, no concept is dependable. That the body is man's outward sheath is undoubtedly correct, but the Bible never confuses spirit and soul as though they are the same. Not only are they different in terms; their very natures differ from each other. The Word of God does not divide man into the two parts of soul and body. It treats man, rather, as tripartite-spirit, soul and body. I Thessalonians 5.23 reads: "May the God of peace himself sanctify you wholly; and may your spirit and soul and body be kept sound and blameless at the coming of our Lord *Jesus Christ.*
>
> This verse precisely shows that we are divided into three parts. The apostle Paul referred here to the complete sanctification of believers, "sanctify you wholly." How is a person wholly sanctified according to the apostle? By his spirit and soul and body being kept. From this, we can easily understand that the whole person comprises these three parts. This verse also makes a distinction between spirit and

47

soul; otherwise, Paul would have said simply "your soul." Since God has distinguished the human spirit from the human soul, we conclude that man is composed of not two, but three, parts; spirit, soul and body.

Is it a matter of any consequence to divide spirit and soul? It is an issue of supreme importance for it affects tremendously the spiritual life of a believer. How can a believer understand spiritual life if he does not know what is the extent of the realm of the spirit? Without such understanding how can he grow spiritually? To fail to distinguish between spirit and soul is fatal to spiritual maturity. Christians often account what is soulical. as spiritual, and thus they remain in a soulish state and seek not what is really spiritual. How can we escape loss if we confuse what God has divided?

Spiritual knowledge is very important to spiritual life. Let us add, however, that it is equally as, if not more, important for a believer to be humble and willing to accept the teaching of the Holy Spirit. If so, the Holy Spirit will grant him the experience of the dividing of spirit and soul, although he may not have too much knowledge concerning this truth. On the one hand, the most ignorant believer, without the slightest idea of the division of spirit and soul, may yet experience such a dividing in real life. On the other hand, the most informed believer, completely conversant with the truth concerning spirit and soul, may nonetheless have no experience of it. Far better is that person who may have both the knowledge and the experience. The majority, however, lack such experience. Consequently, it is well initially to lead these to know the different functions of spirit and soul and then to encourage them to seek what is spiritual.

Other portions of the Scriptures make this same differentiation between spirit and soul. For the word of God is living and active, sharper than any two-edged sword, piercing to the division of soul and spirit of joints and marrow, and discerning the thoughts and intentions of the heart (Heb. 4.12). The writer in this verse divides man's non-corporal elements into two parts, 11 soul and spirit. The corporal part is mentioned here as including the joints and marrow organs of motion and sensation. When the priest uses the sword to cut and completely dissect the sacrifice, nothing inside can be hidden. Even joint and marrow are separated. In like manner the Lord Jesus uses the Word of God on His people to separate thoroughly, to pierce even to the division of the spiritual, the soulical, and the physical. And from this it follows that since soul and spirit can be divided, they must be different in nature. It is thus evident here that man is a composite of three parts." Watchman Nee further explains this difference between the soul and the spirit of man like this.

The Functions of the Spirit, Soul, and Body—Watchman Nee

It is through the corporal body that man comes into contact with the material world. Hence we may label the body as that part which gives us world-consciousness. The soul comprises the intellect, which aids us in the present state of existence, and the emotions, which proceed from the senses. Since the soul belongs to man's own self and reveals his personality, it is termed the part of self-consciousness. The spirit is that part by which we commune with God and by which alone we are able to apprehend and worship Him. Because it tells us of our relationship with God, the spirit is called the element of God-consciousness. God dwells in the spirit, self-dwells in the soul, while senses dwell in the body.

As we have mentioned already, the soul is the meeting point of spirit and body, for there they are merged. By his spirit man holds intercourse with the spiritual world and with the Spirit of God, both receiving and expressing the power and life of the spiritual realm. Through his body man is in contact with the outside sensuous world, affecting it and being is affected by it. The soul stands between these two worlds, yet belongs to both. It is linked with the spiritual world through the spirit and with the material world through the body. It also possesses the power of free will, hence is able to choose from among its environments. The spirit cannot act directly upon the body. It needs a medium, and that medium is the soul produced by the touching of the spirit with the body. The soul therefore stands between the spirit and the body, binding these two together. The spirit can subdue the body through the medium of the soul, so that it will obey God; likewise the body through the soul can draw the spirit into loving the world.

Of these three elements the spirit is the noblest for it joins with God.

The body is the lowest for it contacts with matter. The soul lying between them joins the two together and also takes their character to be its own.

The soul makes it possible for the spirit and the body to communicate and to cooperate. The work of the soul is to keep these two in their proper order so that they may not lose their right relationship ---namely, that the lowest, the body, may be subjected to the spirit, and that the highest, the spirit, may govern the body through the soul. Man's prime factor is definitely the soul. It looks to the spirit to give what the latter has received from the Holy Spirit in order that the soul, after it has been perfected, may transmit what it has obtained to the body; then the body too may share in the perfection of the Holy Spirit and so become a spiritual body.

The spirit is the noblest part of man and occupies the innermost area of his being. The body is the lowest and takes the outermost place. Between these two dwells the soul, serving as their medium. The body is the outer shelter of the soul, while the soul is the outer sheath of the spirit. The spirit transmits its thought to the soul and the soul exercises the body to obey the spirit's order. This is the meaning of the soul as the medium. Before the fall of man the spirit controlled the whole being through the soul.

The power of the soul is most substantial, since the spirit and the body are merged there and make it the site of man's personality and influence. Before man committed sin the power of the soul was completely under the dominion of the spirit. Its strength was therefore the spirit's strength. The spirit cannot itself act upon the body; it can only do so through the medium of the soul. This we can see in Luke 1.46-47: "My soul magnifies the Lord, and my spirit has rejoiced in God my Savior" (Darby). Here the change in tense shows that the spirit first conceived joy in God, and then, communicating with the soul, caused it to give expression to the feeling by means of the bodily organ. (Pember's Earth's Earliest Age)

To repeat, the soul is the site of personality. The will, intellect and emotions of man are there. As the spirit is used to communicate with the spiritual world and the body with the natural world, so the soul stands between and exercises its power to discern and decide whether the spiritual or the natural world should reign. Sometimes too the soul itself takes control over man through its intellect, thus creating an ideational world which reigns. In order for the spirit to govern, the soul must give its consent; otherwise the spirit is helpless to regulate the soul and the body. But this decision is up to the soul, for therein resides the personality of the man.

Actually the soul is the pivot of the entire being, because man's volition belongs to it. It is only when the soul is willing to assume a humble position that the spirit can ever manage the whole man. If the soul rebels against taking such a position the spirit will be powerless to rule. This explains the meaning of the free will of man. Man is not an automaton that turns according to God's will. Rather, man has full sovereign power to decide for himself. He possesses the organ of his own volition and can choose either to follow God's will or to resist Him and follow Satan's will instead. God desires that the spirit, being the noblest part of man, should control the whole being. Yet, the will---the crucial part of individuality-belongs to the soul. It is the will, which determines whether the spirit, the body, or even itself is to rule. In view of the fact that the soul possesses such power and is the organ of man's individuality, the Bible calls man's a living soul."

What a powerful discourse this is from one of my favorite writers, Watchman Nee, who explained the importance of our harnessing our souls. If we don't love God with our souls, our flesh will rule us, not the kingdom of God. Jesus told us, "Love the Lord God with all of your heart, your soul, your mind and your strength." This is righteousness in its infant state.

Jesus said that unless our righteousness exceeded that of the scribes and Pharisees, we wouldn't enter the kingdom of heaven. This statement has a benchmark we must exceed. We must go beyond the threshold of the righteousness of the scribes and Pharisees if we are to achieve heaven. In Isaiah 29:13 (NIV), the Lord said, "These people come near to me with their mouth and honor me with their lips, but their hearts are far from me. Their worship of me is based on merely human rules they have been taught." On another occasion, Jesus said, "This people draweth nigh unto me with their mouth, and honoureth me with their lips; but their heart is far from me." (Matthew 15:8 KJV) that was an indictment! The scribes and Pharisees came near to God with their mouths, looking pious and holy and saying things that sounded spiritual to others. They followed all the religious rules and traditions, but their hearts were not right and pure with God.

If our righteousness is going to exceed this nonsense, we'll have to come under kingdom rule and authority. Our hearts and lips will need to become one so we can give God true heart service. When the communities of God return to really honoring God with their lips, hearts, souls, minds, bodies, and strength, they'll receive what God has for them in the kingdom of God. God has a plan for us to live under his kingdom's rule and authority. A prototype of this kingdom was in the beginning with Adam and Eve in the garden.

Justification and Righteousness

Volumes everywhere teach the doctrine of justification. It sounds so theological and profound, but it's a simple, common-sense doctrine. Justification through Christ means that the moment you accept Jesus Christ as Lord and Savior, something miraculous transpires. Everything you ever did no longer exists; every sin, every mistake, all wrong is wiped clean. Wow! I'm getting as excited as I did the first day I was saved, sanctified, filled with God's precious spirit and under kingdom of God's rule.

- "I, even I, am He that blots out your transgressions for my own sake, and will not remember your sins" (Isaiah 43:25).
- "For I will forgive their iniquity, and I will remember their sin no more" (Jeremiah 31:34).
- "For I will be merciful to their unrighteousness, and their sins and their iniquities will I remember no more" (Hebrews 8:12).
- "And their sins and iniquities will I remember no more" (Hebrews 10:17).

Each of these passages is a declaration that God will forget his people's sins. I have offered four of them here to make the foundation of my thinking on justification firm and adamant. It is written, "In the mouth of two or three witnesses every word shall be established." Here then, you have Isaiah and Jeremiah, two Old Testament prophets, affirming the same thing—is this not enough? Added to these, you have the author of the epistle to the Hebrews, who in all probability was Paul, and these three agree. Their united testimony is that God will forgive completely and remember no more the sins of his people.

Justification means you are not guilty; it's as if you'd never sinned. Your slate is clean! Those in Jesus no longer face condemnation. "If any man be in Christ he is a new creation" (2 Corinthians 5:17); that's kingdom living at its finest. This is the ultimate basis for our existence. We are changed from our old, sinful nature and become new people full of life. We become righteous and have right standing with God. He no longer cares about our past, just our present and future.

People have tried to get me going on my past sins and failures. I boldly look them in the eye with resolve and say, "I don't know what you're talking about." They'll go on: "You remember when you—" I stop them in their tracks. "No, I don't remember." One woman became angry; I saw the spirit of the Devil rise up in her, and I had to rebuke that spirit. Don't let people keep you living in your past; refuse to let them categorize you. You are new; you are justified through Christ. You are declared just, righteous, and holy. Those who accept Jesus Christ as their Lord and Savior become the children of the King and live under the reign of God in his kingdom. In the next chapter, we'll look at this original kingdom of God.

Chapter 9

The Original Kingdom on Earth

> And God said, Let us make man in our image, after
> our likeness: and let them have dominion over the
> fish of the sea, and over the fowl of the air, and over
> the cattle, and over all the earth, and over every
> creeping thing that creepeth upon the earth. So God
> created man in his own image, in the image of God
> created he him; male and female created he them.
> And God blessed them, and God said unto them, Be
> fruitful, and multiply, and replenish the earth, and
> subdue it: and have dominion over the fish of the sea,
> and over the fowl of the air, and over every living
> thing that moveth upon the earth. (Genesis 1:26–28)

Jesus' mission on earth was to reestablish the kingdom of God; he
wanted primarily to restore God's original plan for us. God made
Adam a type of himself and placed him in the garden of Eden to rule
over all earth and all creation. God's original kingdom on earth was
in the garden of Eden, humanity's domain. Adam and Even had it
made! God blessed them and gave them his purpose for existing:
be fruitful and multiply and fill earth.

The earth was void; it didn't even have a form. While in deep meditation one day, I asked the Holy Spirit why earth was empty in the first place. The Holy Spirit began to reveal to me through research and his Word what happened. There was a war in heaven between God and Lucifer.

Lucifer Kicked Out of Heaven

The name Lucifer means "day star" or "son of the morning." Many recognize it as an alternate name of Satan, the fallen angel. But prior to his downfall, Lucifer was a magnificent being with a unique ministry. Unfortunately, pride overtook his heart and sin cost him everything. Lucifer is one of three archangels mentioned in Scripture. God had created him just as he had created all the other angels, but his role was different. Lucifer was referred to as the "covering angel." Just as the cherubim covered the mercy seat of the ark of the covenant, Lucifer was to be the angel of worship, one whose ministry surrounded the heart of heaven. Lucifer was created to dwell eternally in the throne room of heaven, in the presence of God (Ezekiel 28:14).

According to Ezekiel 28:13, a probable reference to Lucifer, we learn that he was an amazing being to behold.

> You were the seal of perfection, full of wisdom and perfect in beauty. You were in Eden, the garden of God; every precious stone was your covering: the sardius, topaz, and diamond, beryl, onyx, and jasper, sapphire, turquoise, and emerald with gold. The workmanship of your timbrels and pipes was prepared for you on the day you were created.

To dwell in the awesome presence of a perfect and holy God, Lucifer had to be perfect. There was nothing ordinary about his appearance. Adorned with gold and precious stones, he truly fit the name "son of the morning." He was a step above the other angels in appearance and intellect. Lucifer's wisdom far exceeded that of other angelic beings, and he understood the ways of God.

But Lucifer's splendor and beauty didn't last. While ministering, he began to consider his own position of prominence. Lucifer became prideful, believing that he deserved more than what he had. He wanted to become like the Most High.

Isaiah 14 reveals the fall of Lucifer from the heights of heaven, which resulted in his status as the creature that he is today.

> How you are fallen from heaven, O Lucifer, son of the morning ... For you have said in your heart: "I will ascend into heaven, I will exalt my throne above the stars of God; I will also sit on the mount of the congregation on the farthest sides of the north; I will ascend above the heights of the clouds, I will be like the Most High."

Lucifer had wisdom, beauty, ability, and perfection, but he wanted more; he wanted to be worshiped like God. But God doesn't share his glory or permit another to receive worship. So before Lucifer had a chance to make his move, he was removed from the presence of God. Cast out of heaven like a bolt of lightning, Lucifer was stripped of his beauty, his position, and his rights to heaven.[9]

The fallen angel ended up on earth and made it a place of absolute desolation and emptiness. Whenever pride against God

---

[9] www.sharefaith.com.

comes in, humanity will always be sent from the presence of God. Watch this. God became lonely in heaven and desired sons and daughters of his own. Remember that a kingdom is nothing without subjects. When God created Adam and Eve to rule in the garden of Eden for eternity, Lucifer got busy trying to stop this dominion God had given Adam and Eve over earth. Jealousy is cruel and will always create rebellion against God. When Lucifer saw the glory God had given humanity, he remembered the glory he once had with God in heaven. God gave Adam instructions to eat of any tree in the garden except that of the Tree of the Knowledge of Good and Evil.

Adam's Reign in Eden

Adam reigned and ruled the garden of Eden as God had intended. He had unlimited fellowship with God 24/7. God gave Adam the monumental task of naming all the animals. Adam was a true ruler of the original kingdom of God on earth. Adam was blessed; God supplied every one of his needs in the garden. There were gold and precious stones in the garden and even a river.

> And a river went out of Eden to water the garden; and from thence it was parted, and became into four heads. The name of the first is Pison: that is it which compasseth the whole land of Havilah, where there is gold; and the gold of that land is good: there is bdellium and the onyx stone. And the name of the second river is Gihon: the same is it that compasseth the whole land of Ethiopia. And the name of the third river is Hiddekel: that is it which goeth toward the east of Assyria. And the fourth river is Euphrates. (Genesis 2:10–14 KJV)

God gave Adam and Eve everything they needed in the garden: "And God said, Behold, I have given you every herb bearing seed, which is upon the face of all the earth, and every tree, in the which is the fruit of a tree yielding seed; to you it shall be for meat" (Genesis 1:29 KJV).

Lies, Trickery, and Deceit

When the enemies of God see his glory in you, when you are blessed by God, watch out! Adam and Eve were ruling God's kingdom on earth in the garden. One day, Lucifer had enough of watching Adam and Eve in fellowship with God and walking with him. Lucifer disguised himself as a beautiful but sneaky serpent and took advantage of an opportunity to deceive Eve. The serpent asked Eve, "Did God tell you not to eat fruit from any tree in the garden?" Eve answered, "God said we could eat any of the fruit from any tree in the garden, except the tree of the knowledge of good and evil. He told us not to eat fruit from that tree or even to touch it. If we do, we will die." "No, you won't!" the serpent replied. "God understands what will happen on the day you eat fruit from that tree. You will see what you have done, and you will know the difference between right and wrong, just as God does."

Eve stared at the fruit. It looked beautiful and tasty. She wanted the wisdom it would give her, and she ate some of it and gave some to Adam to eat. Right away, they saw what they had done, and they realized they were naked. They sewed fig leaves together to cover themselves.

Late in the afternoon, a breeze began to blow, and the man and woman heard God walking in the garden. They were frightened and hid behind trees. The Lord asked, "Adam, where are you?" Adam answered, "I was naked, and when I heard you walking through the garden, I was frightened and hid!" God said to Adam, "How did you know you were naked? Did you eat any fruit from that tree in the middle of the garden?" "It was Eve you put here with me," the man said. "She gave me some of the fruit, and I ate it." God asked Eve, "What have you done?" "The serpent tricked me," she answered. "And I ate some of that fruit." At that moment, Lucifer was given the kingdom of God on earth. Adam and Eve were exiled from it because of their sins. That's why Lucifer is known as the god of this world now.

> Satan, who is the god of this world, has blinded the minds of those who don't believe. They are unable to see the glorious light of the Good News. They don't understand this message about the glory of Christ, who is the exact likeness of God. (2 Corinthians 4:4 NLT)

Adam and Eve had lost the kingdom of God on earth, but God sent his Son in the flesh to redeem humanity and restore the kingdom of God to humanity (Romans 8:3). Preaching the gospel of the kingdom was the main theme of John the Baptist's ministry as the forerunner of Jesus Christ. Even after John was beheaded, Jesus preached, "Repent, for the kingdom of God is at hand."

The garden of Eden was the original kingdom of God on earth, and Jesus' mission was to restore this kingdom to humanity. The stage had been set; the people of God were in captivity, under the rule of the Roman Empire. Jesus taught and preached about this kingdom of God in a subtle way. He taught in parables. In the next chapter, we will examine the significance of parables.

Chapter 10

Parables of the Kingdom of God

And the disciples came, and said unto him, Why
speakest thou unto them in parables?
—Matthew 13:10

Parables are short stories that teach a moral or spiritual lesson. Most of the time, parables are wise, weighty sayings, instructive stories designed to give a deeper understanding of spiritual or heavenly matters in language borrowed from common life.

The disciples asked Jesus why he spoke to the multitudes in parables. Before I give Jesus' answer, we need to understand that the Jews were under the rule of the Roman Empire during this time. Any act of rebellion or treason on their part resulted in major punishment or even death. Jesus Christ was ministering about a politically sensitive matter, the coming of the kingdom of God. This made the leaders of this empire uneasy.

The Pharisees dispatched spies to catch Jesus in anything they could accuse him of. In response to his disciples' question, Jesus said that he wanted people to know and understand the secrets and mysteries of the kingdom of heaven. No doubt some of the leaders of the Roman Empire were there along with the

Pharisees. Jesus gestured in their direction and explained that he didn't want them to learn these secrets. He explained that those who understood these mysteries would receive more spiritual knowledge and grow in it. Jesus said that others were just not going to get it and that those who did would have that understanding taken away from them.

Jesus' communication to the multitudes was a message his real followers would understand and apply while it would simply go over the heads of others. Countries at war use coded messages to keep their secrets from their enemies. This was the same way it was with Jesus Christ; he spoke in parables so the enemies of the kingdom wouldn't understand what he was talking about. Jesus was concealing a message about the kingdom of God.

The Purpose of Parables

Jesus' teaching in parables had a twofold purpose. First, they revealed a teaching; second, they hid the same teaching. That sounds contradictory, but consider the facts surrounding these two purposes. Jesus' parables were usually simple stories that concealed a deeper meaning that those who were in opposition to him wouldn't understand. Parables differ from allegories; whose meanings are not secret or coded so only a select few can understand them. Parables are simple; anyone who seeks for their deeper meaning, their hidden truth, can understand them.

Those who oppose the meaning of a parable won't see its true meaning; they will focus on the story itself. This is true even today. Instead of trying to understand what Jesus was trying to say, many try to decode the story in a fashion that is very similar to allegory. These people will never receive the true meaning of the parable because they aren't looking for it. Those who aren't looking for the meaning of the parable won't discover it. To them, the parable will be simply a nice story.

Parables were meant to explain a Jewish rabbi's point by illustrating it; however, if the point wasn't stated, the parable would amount to no more than a story. Rabbis had some more-secretive teachings that they thought only their closest disciples could handle, and they reserved these for private instruction. Only those who chose to become insiders would understand the meaning of Jesus' parables.

The Parable of the Mustard Seed

> And he said, Whereunto shall we liken the kingdom of God? or with what comparison shall we compare it? It is like a grain of mustard seed, which, when it is sown in the earth, is less than all the seeds that be in the earth: 32 but when it is sown, it groweth up, and becometh greater than all herbs, and shooteth out great branches; so that the fowls of the air may lodge under the shadow of it. (Mark 4:30–32 KJV)

This parable tells us to not look at the size or quantity of what we do. Our ideas may be small at first, but they have the capability to grow into something great. Those who are in the kingdom of God should never minimize small beginnings. Just because something starts off humble doesn't mean it will remain humble. The parable of the mustard seed shows that the beginnings of the gospel may be small, but its end would be much greater. In this way, the work of God's rule in the heart, the kingdom of God within us will carry on. In the soul, where God's rule truly is, it will grow and develop even though at first we cannot imagine it would ultimately produce a massive harvest of great strength.

I've personally witnessed this in the church God had me to plant in Antioch, California, Alllove Faith Church. We started teaching the kingdom of God to alcoholics, drug addicts, prostitutes, liars, thieves, and other broken folk, people to whom other churches wouldn't minister. When they started hearing the gospel of the kingdom, it didn't seem anything was happening to them, but within two years, they became strong believers who stopped the sin business and were living under the rule of the kingdom of God in their hearts.

On another occasion, the church was worshiping in schools, hotels—any place we could. We didn't have a church home. God took me to an abandoned office complex and told me to drive into the parking lot. I walked through the complex, a ghost town. God told me in my spirit to call those things that were not as though they already were. I stood in the courtyard of the complex and said, "Father, you said you would give us every place the soles of our feet shall tread upon."

Months later, in December 2012, we moved into this 26,000-square-foot complex on two acres; this was at a time when we had only $600 in our treasury. Our offer of almost $1.6 million for the property was accepted even though our treasury had gone down to $325. God had placed real estate investors and people in our lives to give us the money to buy and renovate it. We then leased some space to nonprofit community organizations. Now, the property is paying for itself.

I sowed the Word of God on that day in the parking lot, and months later, we owned it. To God is the glory. That is a perfect example of the kingdom of God taking something small and making it grow magnificently.

Little is much in the kingdom of God. When God starts ruling, anything is possible. Look at the pictures of the kingdom of God moving for us.

The Parable of the Leaven

> Another parable spake he unto them; The kingdom of heaven is like unto leaven, which a woman took, and hid in three measures of meal, till the whole was leavened. (Matthew 13:33)

The *Matthew Henry Commentary on the Bible* reads,

> The preaching of the gospel works like leaven in the hearts of those who receive it. The leaven works certainly, so does the word, yet gradually. It works silently, and without being seen, yet strongly; without noise, for so is the way of the Spirit, but without fail. Thus it was in the world. The apostles, by preaching the gospel of the kingdom, hid a handful of leaven in the great mass of mankind. It was made powerful by the Spirit of the Lord of hosts, who works, and none can hinder. Thus it is in the heart. When the gospel comes into the soul, it works a thorough change; it spreads itself into all the powers and faculties of the soul, and alters the property even of the members of the body, (Romans 6:13). From these parables we are taught to expect a gradual progress; therefore let us inquire, are we growing in grace? and in holy principles and habits?

The Parable of the Treasure

This parable compares the kingdom of God to hidden treasure in a field; it's one of my favorites. How many times have you hidden something valuable but forgot where you hid it? Someone else comes along and finds it; your loss becomes his or her gain. It reminds me of a story about a family that owned 480 acres. They had been trying to sell the property because it involved too much work and made too little money.

One day while working in the field, a hired worker spotted oil in a far corner of the land. He immediately sold all he had and purchased the land from those who said it was too much work. The worker became very wealthy because he struck oil. That sounds a lot like Jesus' parable. The worker kept quiet about the oil and was joyful about it; he sold everything he had and became wealthy.

God is looking for people who will sell out to him in every aspect. God wants our hearts, minds, bodies, and souls. We'll never lose in the kingdom of God, which is greater than any oil field. Everything we need is in the kingdom of God.

The Parable of the Pearl

> Again, the kingdom of heaven is like unto a merchant man, seeking goodly pearls. (Matthew 13:45)

Jesus compared the kingdom of God to priceless pearls. This parable discusses a merchant who sought pearls and found one very valuable pearl. Like the man who found treasure in the field, he sold all he had to purchase the pearl.

Jesus Christ is the priceless pearl, and just like the merchant, when you find Jesus and let him into your heart, you need to sell everything you have to allow Jesus Christ, the King of Kings, to rule your life. The kingdom of God is all about allowing God to rule your mind, your actions—everything.

Jesus was creating a new culture in Jerusalem. His teaching about this kingdom of God "philosophy" was profound; it was a new way of thinking. You would think that with all the results Jesus obtained that people today would be teaching the kingdom of God.

Chapter 11

The Kingdom of God Revealed

For the kingdom of God is not meat and drink; but
righteousness, and peace, and joy in the Holy Ghost.
—Romans 14:17 KJV

This Scripture starts out by explaining what the kingdom of God is
not; it's not just eating, drinking, and having a good time. Many kings
of old would throw huge feast and celebrations in their kingdoms
with eating, dancing, and drinking. The king would sometimes get
so drunk that he would offer half his kingdom just for the asking.

King Herod once threw a party for his high officials, military
commanders, and all the leading men of Galilee. During the party,
the daughter of Herodias, King Herod's brother's wife, whom he had
married, came to the party and danced before the king. I imagine
the king was royally intoxicated and full of himself. It's told that
when she danced, she pleased the king and his guest so much that
the king told her, "Ask me for anything you want, and I will give it
to you." The King made an oath: "Whatever you ask I will give you,
up to half of my kingdom." His word was law.

The girl asked her mother what she should ask for. The mother,
seeking revenge against John the Baptist because he had publicly

stated, "It is not lawful for you to have your brother's wife," sent word through her daughter: "I want the head of John." Because the word of the king was very powerful and he had made an oath, regardless of his frame of mind, it became law. The king was greatly distressed but didn't want to refuse her in front of his guests. He sent an executioner with orders to bring back John's head.

The man beheaded John in the prison and brought back his head on a platter. He presented it to the girl, and she gave it to her mother. What a travesty resulted from all that drinking.

Many kings and world leaders have made life-changing decisions during times of eating and drinking. I don't know for sure, but Paul, being the scholar he was, maybe had had this on his mind when he made the statement that the kingdom of God contrasted with the kingdom of man was not one of meat and drink.

What is the kingdom of God? It is first righteousness. In the last chapter, we discussed righteousness in detail, but I'll present more on it here. Righteousness is believing God; it's trusting what God says. God promised Abraham that he would become the father of many nations. The problem was that Abraham was old and Sarah, his wife, was barren. But Abraham took God at his word.

Years later, Abraham received his son. Galatians 3:6 tells us, "So also Abraham believed God, and it was credited to him as righteousness." Abraham's belief in God gave him right standing, righteousness, with God. Every time we believe God and take him at his word, we receive right standing with him. The kingdom of God begins with righteousness. We must present our bodies as living sacrifices that are holy and acceptable to God through our service (Romans 12:1). When we come to God, we must believe he rewards those who diligently seek him (Hebrews 11:6).

When you understand the righteousness of God, the condemnation the Enemy tries to enslave you with will no longer work. It's better to have righteousness than to be outside the will of God. Righteousness exalts a nation, but sin condemns any people. The King James Version says sin is a reproach to any people. A kingdom and sin cannot coexist; that would be like having light and dark in the same room at the same time; it's either one or the other.

One popular culture or philosophy that is festering today tells us it's all right to be of the world, unrighteousness, and still be in the kingdom of God. I beg to differ. It is written,

> Love not the world, neither the things that are in the world. If any man love the world, the love of the Father is not in him. For all that is in the world, the lust of the flesh, and the lust of the eyes, and the pride of life, is not of the Father, but is of the world. And the world passeth away, and the lust thereof: but he that doeth the will of God abideth forever. (1 John 2:15–17)

If the love of the Father is not in you, his kingdom cannot rule in your life. Righteousness and unrighteousness just won't hang out together.

> For every one that doeth evil hateth the light, neither cometh to the light, lest his deeds should be reproved. But he that doeth truth cometh to the light that his deeds may be made manifest, that they are wrought in God. (John 3:20–21)

You cannot walk in unrighteousness and be a part of the kingdom of God.

No Inheritance in the Kingdom

Years ago, I was backsliding; I was doing everything bad you could imagine. My life was sinful. I was miserable but didn't want anything to do with God. I won't go into graphic details about my actions; just know that I was out there. But some Scriptures changed my life seemingly overnight. I learned that when you're unrighteous, you have no inheritance in the kingdom of God; you have nothing coming to you. Galatians 5:19–21 (NIV) tells us,

> The acts of the flesh are obvious: sexual immorality, impurity and debauchery; idolatry and witchcraft; hatred, discord, jealousy, fits of rage, selfish ambition, dissensions, factions and envy; drunkenness, orgies, and the like. I warn you, as I did before, that those who live like this will not inherit the kingdom of God.

That blew me away. I realized I wouldn't inherit the kingdom of God, and from that day forward, I got rid of everything that was not godly. You can do this too. "What does it profit a man to gain the whole world and to lose his soul?" Right standing with God will place you in the position to have divine favor on your life.

When you are righteous and the kingdom of God is ruling your life, you'll walk in the kingdom in peace and know the peace of God that passes all understanding. Joy, a spiritual force, is one of the fruits of the spirit. Joy comes from the Holy Spirit when you have totally surrendered yourself to the will of the kingdom of God. The kingdom of God is righteous, peaceful, and joyous in the Holy Spirit.

Chapter 12

The Kingdom of God and Abundance

Thank God if your knowledge about his kingdom has increased. The most exciting part of this is even though a real kingdom is coming, God's plan to rule your life started before you were born. God wants you to live a life of abundance.

Many think their abundance is measured only by material gain and wealth, but once you examine the Scriptures closely, you'll see that "wealth" takes many forms. Many movements today focus on only one aspect—what you can gain materially by your relationship with God. This narrow-minded thinking has caused many to live beneath their privileges in other areas of life.

Now is a great time to deal with the areas of abundance the kingdom of God will bring forth when you allow it to rule. In 1 John 3:2 (KJV), we read, "Beloved, I wish above all things that thou mayest prosper and be in health, even as thy soul prospereth." Prosperity consists of more than material matters. This Scripture deals with health and the prospering of the soul. In the Amplified Version, this passage reads, "Beloved, I pray that you may prosper in every way and [that your body] may keep well, even as [I know] your soul keeps well *and* prospers."

Your body will be kept well when your soul prospers. As your soul goes, so does your health. Once your soul comes under kingdom rule, your health will follow. Let us look closer at this. Jesus said, "The thief cometh not but to kill steal and to destroy, but I have come that you might have life and it more abundantly" (John 10:10 KJV); "The thief comes only in order to steal and kill and destroy. I came that they may have *and* enjoy life, and have it in abundance (to the full, till it overflows)" (John 10:10 Amplified). God wants you to prosper in health, life, and abundance until it fills you up and it overflows. God's plan was not for you to barely make it in life or to be broken down mentally and disgusted. God means for you to live in total victory in all your doings.

Once you come under divine kingdom authority, once you submit to the King's will and allow him to make the best decisions for you, prosperity and success will overtake you. Jesus spoke on another occasion and told you to get rid of fear: "Fear not, little flock; for it is your Father's good pleasure to give you the kingdom" (Luke 12:32 KJV). Another writer put it like this: "For God hath not given us the spirit of fear; but of power, and of love, and of a sound mind." (2Timothy 1:7 KJV)

No Peace, No Prosperity

Life is full of situations that keep us from abiding in peace. The suggestion that peace and prosperity walk hand in hand is absolute. Peace is a state of tranquility, quiet, and calm. Peace is an important element of prosperity; Jeremiah wrote, "And you have removed my soul far off from peace: I forgot prosperity" (Lamentations 3:17).

During the prophet Jeremiah's plight when the Chaldeans were besieging Jerusalem, he communicated the depressed and discouraging part of his experience. His soul was far from peace, which wasn't in sight. During his trial, the Lord became appalling to him. Jeremiah's situation was melancholy in itself; the lack of peace makes the cup of lack a bitter cup. Jeremiah had forgotten how it felt to be in a state of peace, and he lost consciousness of prosperity. He wrestled with anguish and fear, which will always produce a harvest of unbelief. His struggle between unbelief and faith was often severe. Because of the condition of his soul, he forgot prosperity.

As long as life burdens you, as long as you allow its circumstances to dictate your mental state, you won't know prosperity. When you struggle with believing God and standing in faith, you won't be at peace, and where there's no peace, there's no prosperity.

On one occasion, Jesus was summoned to Jarius's home to pray for his dying daughter. Jesus was detained by another woman who had been battling an issue of blood for twelve years. She touched Jesus' garment and was made whole. But while Jesus was delayed by this, Jarius's daughter died. When the Savior finally arrival at Jarius's home, he found mourners weeping and wailing. Jesus told them that the girl was just sleeping, but they scorned him. This was anything but a peaceful situation due to the weeping and the doubters' laughter at Jesus. Jesus refused to work under those conditions; he knew the value of peace and its connection to prosperity. Jesus sent everybody out—mourners, those laughing, and doubters alike. When Jesus was in his element and alone with his Father, he prayed for the daughter, and she awoke.

Chapter 13

Kingdom Wisdom

Possibility and manifestation are the fruits of the divine nature of Christ in you. Did you know you have the power of creation? This is not church related or a matter of congregational teaching; this is a fact.

So many times due to a mixture of church rhetoric and false teaching, people come up with a system that's more confusing to the people of God than anything else. We were created in the image of God and after his likeness. We are just like our creator; the sooner we believe this, the better off we'll be.

We have struggled with our identity for years and created religion as a means of getting back to God's divine nature. Let me say this: let go and let Christ. We discussed earlier the significance of being righteous in the sight of God. Yes, there is a divine nature that powers you and makes you go. Medical science tells us the electrical current that makes the heart pump comes from and unknown source. I want you to think in terms of an absolute presence of a spiritual being inside you.

It's common to find silent partners involved in a business who supply the capital for ventures. We have a silent partner in Christ, who resides in us. This is why being born again is so vital to our success. Have you ever wondered why we can desire something and think on it with passion consistently and it manifests in the physical? We have the power of creation within us because of who we are. For all our lives, we have been facing the challenge of defeating God's enemies who don't want us develop into the creations God intends us to be. Our enemies constantly try to distract us and keep us off focus.

Paul wrote about this to the Colossians. I quote the Amplified Version here to help shed light on Christ, our essential silent partner: "To whom God was pleased to make known how great for the Gentiles are the riches of the glory of this mystery, which is Christ within and among you, the Hope of [realizing the] glory" (Colossians 1:27).

God wants us to know ourselves so we can become familiar with this mystery. God wants us to receive kingdom revelation on this very important matter. After we are born again, our original nature takes over. Most people don't know they have a silent partner in Christ, so they try to coexist with their old natures in thinking, everyday life, and living. John the Baptist said, "I must decrease and Christ must increase" (John 3:30), and this has deep spiritual revelation and connotation. When we decrease our fleshly nature, his divinity will begin to reign and rule. This explains why when we fast, something supernatural happens. Isaiah 58 tells us that fasting loosens the bonds of wickedness. Fasting will undo the heavy burdens put on us by the enemies of God and break every yoke. Fasting will cause us to die in the flesh. Once we die in the flesh, we are no longer living; Christ in us is living, thinking, reigning, and ruling.

Let's look at what really happens when man decreases, by yielding to the will of the spirit or Christ in him. "I am crucified with Christ: nevertheless I live; yet not I, but Christ liveth in me: and the life which I now live in the flesh I live by the faith of the Son of God, who loved me, and gave himself for me" (Galatians 2:20). *Crucified* here means put to death. Paul was saying he had been put to death in the flesh but he was still living. It was no longer Paul living but Christ living in him; he was living by his faith of the Son of God.

The Christ in you knows all and sees all. He's been there and done that. When you allow Christ in you to make decisions in family, marriage, business, and everyday matters, you'll get on top and stay there. You'll become the head, not the tail; you'll be above, never below. The Christ in you has your best interests at heart; he wants you to excel and succeed in everything you do.

You will have to communicate with Christ inside. I communicate with him daily. But I don't want you to confuse this communication with ceremonial prayer. Intimacy is vital here. You can ask Christ anything, but don't be alarmed when you receive a response.

> And he said, Go forth, and stand upon the mount before the LORD. And, behold, the LORD passed by, and a great and strong wind rent the mountains, and brake in pieces the rocks before the LORD; but the LORD was not in the wind: and after the wind an earthquake; but the LORD was not in the earthquake:
>
> And after the earthquake a fire; but the LORD was not in the fire: and after the fire a still small voice.
>
> And it was so, when Elijah heard it, that he wrapped his face in his mantle, and went out, and stood in the entering in of the cave. And, behold, there came a voice unto him, and said, What doest thou here, Elijah? (1 Kings 19:11–13 KJV)

People often look for something spectacular to happen during their communications with the Lord, but he doesn't always part our Red Seas as he did for Moses. We look for the dramatic and miss the simple. In Elijah's case, when the Lord passed by, high winds hit the mountains and even broke rocks into pieces. The Lord was not in the wind! After the wind came an earthquake, but the Lord was not in the earthquake either. After the earthquake came a fire, but the Lord wasn't in it. The Lord's voice was still and small.

Your essential silent partner, Christ, is waiting for you to settle down and listen to the eternal wisdom he wants to share with you, but you could be too busy. Once you allow Christ to reign and rule in you, the kingdom of God will take over all your affairs and govern your mind.

Why wouldn't you want someone who has been here forever to regulate your mind? Haven't you tried it your way long enough? Get out of the way and let his mind be in you (Philippians 2:5).

God's Divine Nature in Us

Have you ever wondered how you became you? Have you ever considered what it means that you were created in his image? God said, "Let us make man in our image" (Genesis 1:26). God made us in the image of himself, Christ, and the Holy Spirit. What I'm about to tell you is controversial; it goes against what you've been taught, but prayerfully consider it. Only those who are open to the concept of the kingdom of God ruling will grasp this. Scripture tells us God breathed life into us to make us living souls, and what he breathed into us was his Spirit.

Let me define *image*, a subject that has been all over the map and around the corner twice and then some. An image is a reproduction or imitation of the form of a person or thing; it's the optical counterpart of an object produced by perhaps a lens or mirror.[10] Some Bible students have tried to make a distinction between "image" and "likeness." Image has been considered our essential nature as God's special creation, and likeness has been thought of in terms of our reflecting his goodness, grace, and love. They maintain that humanity in the fall retained God's image but lost his likeness.

The two words, however, seem to identify the same divine act. The repetition represents the Hebrew literary style of parallelism used for emphasis. The Hebrew *selem*, "image," refers to a hewn or carved image (1 Samuel 6:5; 2 Kings 11:18) like a statue, which bears a strong physical resemblance to whatever it represents. The Hebrew *demuth*, "likeness," means a facsimile. Compare 2 Kings 16:10, "fashion" or "pattern" (NAS), "sketch" (NIV, REB), and "exact model" (TEV). Neither of the words implies that we are divine, but we were endowed with some of God's characteristics; there is a likeness but not a sameness.[11]

I've watched the San Francisco Giants play ball. In front of the stadium, on Willie Mays Way, sits a statue of hall of famer Willie Mays. The statue is a replica of him, but it's not him. In this way, we are replicas of God, but we're not God. The way many people try to lord it over others as God perplexes me.

Let's look at something else in the Scriptures that is profound. When Adam fell and was expelled from the garden, Scripture didn't say Adam became a God. It states in Genesis 3:22, "The LORD God said, Behold, the man is become as one of us, to know good and evil: and now, lest he put forth his hand, and take also of the tree of life, and eat, and live forever." Humans didn't become God; they don't

---

10 *Merriam-Webster Dictionary.*
11 *Holman Bible Dictionary.*

have the authority or knowledge to complicate life by attempting to lord it over other humans; this is where conflict comes from.

Humans attempted to do something they hadn't been designed to do. God had given Adam and Eve dominion over earth and all creatures. We are special, unique creations, but that doesn't make us God. The psalmist asked, "What is man?" (Psalm 8:4). Intellectuals through the ages have attempted to untangle the mystery of that statement. Philosophers, theologians, psychologists, and anthropologists have constantly explored that topic. All have realized that the human being "is fearfully and wonderfully made" (Psalm 139:14).

Examining Psalm 8, we see that humanity was made a little lower than angels and has been crowned with glory and honor, but that still does not make us God.

This is where you'll start having problems with this writing. Psalm 82 states that God is standing in the congregation of the mighty and is judging among the gods. I call these gods here the little gods, the children of the most high God. "For we are God's masterpiece. He has created us anew in Christ Jesus, so we can do the good things he planned for us long ago" (Ephesians 2:10). The psalmist asked in Psalms 82 (KJV), "How long will you judge unjustly and accept the persons of the wicked?" Scripture talks about how humans constantly made bad decisions walking around in darkness. "I have said you are God's, (Psalms 82 KJV) (John 10:34 KJV) however because you constantly make the wrong decisions you will die like men and fall like one of the princes." We are a prototype of God, but we are not almighty. We have the power of creation as God does. We can makes things, including impressive works of art. Poets, writers, philosophers, and lawyers make things with ideas and the compelling use of words. Doctors make people healthier. Manufacturers make things with raw materials; chefs make things with fruits, vegetables, meats, and spices. We all have the ability to create things. We have attributes of God, but once again, we are not God.

We can create with our thoughts and words. Let me qualify this statement. Proverbs states that as we think, so are we (Proverbs 23:7). What we think in our hearts will manifest itself in the physical world. Death and life are in the power of the tongue, and those who love it will eat the fruit of that harvest.

But with all this ability and ingenuity, we're still not God. If we were, we'd have no need for a God and his kingdom to reign in our lives. Jesus Christ would not have put emphasis on this good news of the kingdom. Yes, we have godlike attributes and characteristics, but we cannot rule ourselves. Once we are on the verge of annihilating earth, God will step in to stop us from destroying ourselves and earth. That will set the stage for God's eternal kingdom to reign and rule forever.

The Holy Spirit

Jesus Christ spoke to his disciples about the work of the Holy Spirit during his last days on earth. He opened his heart with compelling love and poured out his soul. Jesus talked to the disciples as a father would to his family before departing earth. During my own father's last days on earth, he would call me into his room—just the two of us—and tell me what I should expect as his son and how to take care of my mother. He went on and on about my not choosing sides with my sisters and the rest of the family but remaining neutral and independent in my decision making.

Jesus spoke to his disciples as friends and gave them full insight into the work of the Holy Spirit after he went back to his Father. He laid out the complete plan of the Holy Spirit on earth in John 14–16.

The Holy Spirit is extremely important to the kingdom of God and how it operates in the lives of believers. Let us observe the relationship of the Holy Spirit and how it prepares to lead us into the eternal kingdom of God, which is soon to come: "And I will pray the Father, and he shall give you another Comforter, that he may abide with you forever" (John 14:16).

The disciples had walked with Jesus daily for three years and had witnessed miracles, healing, and deliverance. Jesus was preparing his disciples for his ascension to his Father. He was making it clear to them that the Holy Spirit would take his place in the very people with whom he had walked on earth. He let them know the Spirit would give them the strength they would need to undergo the trials and persecutions they would endure on behalf of the kingdom he had brought into the world. The stage was set for the world to experience the kingdom because the Son of God had preached the gospel of the kingdom of God to the multitudes.

Jesus would soon leave them. They would need the Comforter to take his place. This term comes from the Greek *parákletos*, "a counselor, a helper, an intercessor, an advocate, a strengthener, or a standby." The New Testament Greek word is composed of two common words: *pára*, "alongside of," like two parallel lines, and *kaléo*, "to call." Brought together, they make one word that means someone called alongside another.

The Holy Spirit is the third person of the Godhead, the divine nature, the essence of God.[12] God has three distinct persons or characteristics—God the Father, God the Son, and God the Holy Spirit. The *Holman Bible Dictionary* explains these terms. *Godhead* is a theological term used to define God as an undivided unity expressed in the threefold nature of the Father, Son, and Holy Spirit.

---

[12] *Merriam-Webster Dictionary, Holman Bible Dictionary.*

A distinctly Christian doctrine, the Trinity is considered a divine mystery beyond human comprehension to be reflected upon only through scriptural revelation. The Trinity is a biblical concept that expresses the dynamic character of God, not a Greek idea pressed into Scripture from philosophical or religious speculation. While the word *trinity* doesn't appear in Scripture, the Trinitarian structure appears throughout the New Testament to affirm that God is manifested through Jesus Christ by means of the Spirit.

A proper biblical view of the Trinity balances the concepts of unity and distinctiveness. Two errors concerning this doctrine are tritheism and unitarianism. Tritheism emphasizes the distinctiveness of the Godhead to the point that the Trinity is seen as three separate gods, polytheism. Unitarianism excludes the concept of their distinctiveness while focusing solely on the aspect of God the Father. In this way, Christ and the Holy Spirit are placed in lower categories and made less than divine. Both errors compromise the effectiveness and contribution of God's activity in redemptive history.

The Holy Spirit is God manifested as a counselor to all who require guidance. The Holy Spirit gives supreme advice in all matters of life, especially in the kingdom of God. At many times, I didn't know exactly what I should do, so I simply went before the Lord in prayer alone and waited patiently for his instruction.

The Holy Spirit is an intercessor. Paul said it like this in Romans 8:26: "Likewise the Spirit also helpeth our infirmities: for we know not what we should pray for as we ought; but the Spirit itself maketh intercession for us with groaning's which cannot be uttered."

We have an advocate in the Holy Spirit; he pleads our cause to God the Father, reminding him that we are his workmanship created in his image. The Holy Spirit reminds the Father that we are heirs of God and joint heirs with Christ Jesus. Sometimes, we don't act as though we belong to the Father, but the Holy Spirit goes to God on our behalf anyway. It is written, "My little children, there things I write unto you, that ye sin not. And if any man sin, we have an advocate with the Father, Jesus Christ the righteous" (1 John 2:1).

Jesus said the comforter would come, and the comforter is there when we mess up and make bad decisions. The Holy Spirit is there to heal us everywhere we hurt. The Holy Spirit will reprove the world of sin, of righteousness, and of judgment. When we are reproved, we are corrected. Jesus said the Holy Spirit "will reprove of sin, because they believe not on me, of righteousness because I go to my Father, and you see me no more; of judgment, because the prince of this world is judged" (John 16:9–10).

The Holy Spirit is the Spirit of truth and will guide always to the truth. The Holy Spirit does not speak of himself; but whatsoever he shall hear, that shall he speak: and he will show you things to come. The Holy Spirit shall glorify Jesus because he receives from him and he will reveal it to you (John 16:13–14).

My friend, the Holy Spirit is a vital source for all believers pertaining to the kingdom of God. We are dealing with an Enemy we cannot see, but the Holy Spirit sees and knows all. He gives us the wisdom to wait patiently for the coming of the physical kingdom of God. I know up until this time we have discussed the internal, invisible kingdom of God, but a real kingdom is coming that will supersede all the kingdoms of this world.

I could write so much more about the Holy Spirit, but time will not allow me. I encourage you to receive the Holy Spirit in you as a gift from God. God wants you to have this gift, and receiving it is very important to life in the kingdom of God. After you have been born again by having accepted Jesus Christ as your Savior, completely turn your heart, will, and soul over to God. Don't do anything that is ungodly. Ask the Holy Spirit to come into your life, and let him in. When you ask the Holy Spirit to reign and rule in your life, expect it will happen by the faith of Jesus Christ. Christ is in you, and you no longer live by your faith but by the faith of Jesus Christ in you.

Chapter 14

The Physical Kingdom of God

When we think in terms of something being real, we think in terms of it being fixed, permanent, such as a building. Real is not artificial, fraudulent, or illusory but genuine! We have outlined the kingdom of God as an invisible kingdom throughout this book. I received the title for this book as an inspiration from God. Though a real kingdom is coming, this doesn't mean the kingdoms of this world are false kingdoms, but they are temporary kingdoms, forerunners of the eternal kingdom. From childhood on, I was taught the kingdom of God is heaven, but I found out that wasn't true. I'll outlined Scripture after Scripture to show you the physical kingdom of God Jesus Christ spoke about when he was on this earth. Before you throw this book against the wall and say I'm blaspheming, hold on until I reveal some things to you. When I first received the revelation from God, I was thrown for a loop. I went to several elders, bishops, even priests, and they all told me to never preach this, that it was not the time. They would agree with me only to tell me to keep it quiet. Well, here is the revelation that God has shown me.

Daniel's Revelation

A long time ago, God gave a Jewish prophet named Daniel a special revelation of future world administrations. While he was serving in the court of Nebuchadnezzar, the king of Babylon, God revealed to Daniel that there would be world-ruling empires following the Babylonian empire—the Persian, Greek, and Roman empires. Daniel was motivated to write,

> And in the days of these kings the God of heaven will set up a kingdom which shall never be destroyed; and the kingdom shall not be left to other people; it shall break in pieces and consume all these kingdoms, and it shall stand forever. (Daniel 2:44)

Daniel added that the saints of the Most High would take the kingdom and would possess this world-ruling kingdom—God's kingdom—which would stand forever (Daniel 7:18). Daniel wrote that the enemies of God would wage war against the saints and would prevail until God judged the saints and the saints possessed the kingdom (Daniel 7:22).

The parallel to this Scripture is in Revelation 13:7, "and it was given unto him to make war with the saints, and to overcome them: and power was given him over all kindreds, and tongues, and nations."

Look at Daniel 7:27: "And the kingdom and dominion, and the greatness of the kingdom under the whole heaven, shall be given to the people of the saints of the Most High, whose kingdom is an everlasting kingdom, and all dominions shall serve and obey him."

Based on what Daniel wrote, the kingdom of God will be set up on earth and other earthly kingdoms will come to an end. This prophesied kingdom will not be invisible or simply a philosophical movement that dwells in us or in our midst through Jesus Christ. Instead, by the hand of God, it will be a literal kingdom with territory, (earth) a ruler, (Jesus Christ), laws (the Laws of God), and subjects (the saints of the most high God) that will rule over all the nations on earth.

When Jesus was on earth and preaching the good news of the kingdom of God, the world-ruling kingdoms prophesied by Daniel hadn't completed their individual assignments. Humanity hadn't determined it was incapable of ruling and governing itself. It wasn't time for God's kingdom to replace all human governments. Jesus told Pilate, "My kingdom is not of this world. If My kingdom were of this world, my servants would fight, so that I should not be delivered to the Jews; but now my kingdom is not from here" (John 18:36).

The kingdom of God hadn't appeared on earth, but that didn't stop Jesus' disciples from asking questions about it. Jesus had taught them to pray for this kingdom to come and make it their priority (Matthew 6:10, 33). Curious about this kingdom, the disciples asked Jesus, "Tell us, when these things will be? And what will be the sign of your coming, and of the end of the age?" (Matthew 24:3). Jesus told them there would be false prophets, wars, famines, pestilences, and earthquakes. But "the end will not come immediately," he said (Luke 21:9). These events were just "the beginning of sorrows" (Matthew 24:8).

When he talked about these matters with his disciples after his resurrection, Jesus again affirmed that the prophesied kingdom was not yet on earth (Acts 1:3–8). He referred to "times or seasons" that were under the control of the Father. Understanding the broad expanse of human history as no human can, God the Father will decide when to send Jesus to establish the kingdom of God on earth (Matthew 24:36; Mark 13:32). In Acts 1, Jesus told his disciples they needed to expand their understanding of the time God was taking to work with humanity.

I believe God has allowed time to pass during which "firstfruits"—an initially small group of people—would be called and trained to serve as teachers when Jesus returns to earth to set up the kingdom (James 1:18; Revelation 5:10). This will happen after the events prophesied by John in Revelation. Then Christ will appear. After the seventh angel sounds, loud voices in heaven will then finally say, "The kingdoms of this world have become the kingdoms of our Lord and of His Christ, and He shall reign forever and ever!" (Revelation 11:15).

Enter the Real Kingdom

After the tribulation period, after the saints of the most high God have been raptured, earth and humanity will experience events that will lead to their near annihilation. "heaven will open, and a white horse shall appear, and the rider on the horse was called Faithful and True, and in righteousness he will judge and make war. His eyes were as a flame of firs, and on his head were many crowns; and he had a name written, that no man knew, but he himself. He was clothed with a vesture dipped in blood: and his name is called The Word of God"(Revelation 19:11–14 KJV). Under the leadership of the antichrist, the beast and the world powers will be on the verge of destroying themselves with nuclear weapons of mass destruction. At that time, Jesus will step in an avert this destruction by defeating them. The antichrist system will be overthrown, and Satan will be cast into the bottomless pit for a thousand years (Revelation 20:1–2).

"And I saw a new heaven and a new earth: for the first heaven and the first earth were passed away; and there was no more sea"

(Revelation 21:1). The part that startles me is in the second verse of this same chapter: "And I John saw the holy city, New Jerusalem, coming down from God out of heaven." Are you getting this? Coming down from God out of heaven! We are not going to heaven; heaven is coming to us! It goes on to say, "The tabernacle of God is with men, and he will dwell with them, and they shall be his people, and God himself shall be with them, and be their God." To further validate this kingdom coming to earth, look at Revelation 21:10: "And he carried me away in the spirit to a great and high mountain, and showed me that great city, the holy Jerusalem, descending out of heaven from God."

A tabernacle is a tent or sanctuary, a house of worship. God's tabernacle is with humans just as it was in the garden of Eden. God dwelled with humanity in Eden and will do so in the kingdom of God. If the New Jerusalem is descending out of heaven from God, that means it's coming down here to earth.

The next verses of Revelation 21 begin to describe this new city in great detail; there will be no sun, neither of the moon for the glory of God did lighten it and the Lamb is the light thereof (Revelation 21:23). The saved nations will walk in the light of this new kingdom. The kings of earth are even going to bring their glory and honor into it.

My friend, the kingdom of God Jesus was teaching and preaching about was this kingdom, the new heaven and the new earth. This kingdom shall reign for eternity. All of God's goodness, greatness, and mercy will rule this kingdom. This will be a real kingdom. Live your life in such a way that you will experience this kingdom soon to come in its fullness. I live in anticipation of this kingdom coming on the scene. Oh what a relief it will be!

Chapter 15

The Kingdom of God by Grace

Therefore it is of faith that it might be according to grace,
so that the promise might be sure to all the seed, not only
to those who are of the law, but also to those who are
of the faith of Abraham, who is the father of us all.
—Romans 4:16 NKJV

The realization of the kingdom of God is from your faith in God and the sacred things of God. Have faith in God and his Word; "But without faith it is impossible to please Him, for he who comes to God must believe that He is, and that He is a rewarder of those who diligently seek Him" (Hebrews 11:6 NKJV). You can give recognition to the kingdom of God only when you give special notice or attention to it. The kingdom of God is definitely a real kingdom that is waiting to rule your life today.

Nicodemus, who was a ruler of the Jews, a Pharisee, and a member of the Sanhedrin council, visited Jesus at night for fear of seeming to be in collusion with Jesus Christ. He called Jesus "rabbi," master or teacher, and said no man could do the miracles Jesus did without God being with him. Jesus gave him insight and the way into the kingdom of God when he said that unless someone is born of water and of Spirit, that person couldn't enter the kingdom of God.

Baptism is an ordinance of the church that needs to be reestablished. Baptismal pools in most churches are rusting away and used for storage. Baptism was important in Jesus' time; when he was baptized by John the Baptist, God descended on him in the form of a dove. When Jesus was born of water and of Spirit, the kingdom of God (as we discussed in earlier chapters) began to reign and rule in the life of Jesus. At that moment, he entered the kingdom of God and the kingdom of God entered him.

Don't say that Jesus was the Son of God and had come to earth with it, because he didn't. He was born of a virgin; he took on the form of man. Philippians 2:7(KJV) says, but made himself of no reputation, taking the form of a bondservant, *and* coming in the likeness of men.

Unless we repent, turn away from sin, and accept Jesus Christ into our hearts, we won't be able to enter the kingdom of God. The sacred things of God cannot and will not dwell in the midst of an unclean temple. In 1 Corinthians 6:15–20 (NKJV), we read,

> Know ye not that your bodies are the members of Christ? shall I then take the members of Christ, and make them the members of an harlot? God forbid.

> What? know ye not that he which is joined to an harlot is one body? for two, saith he, shall be one flesh.

> But he that is joined unto the Lord is one spirit.

Flee fornication. Every sin that a man doeth is
without the body; but he that committeth fornication
sinneth against his own body.

What? know ye not that your body is the temple of
the Holy Ghost which is in you, which ye have of God,
and ye are not your own?
For ye are bought with a price: therefore glorify God
in your body, and in your spirit, which are God's.

Entrance into the kingdom of God is by faith first "that if you
confess with your mouth the Lord Jesus and believe in your heart
that God has raised Him from the dead, you will be saved" (Romans
10:9 NKJV). You believe in God's righteousness in your heart and
express that verbally! Paul said it like this: "And since we have
the same spirit of faith, according to what is written, 'I believed
and therefore I spoke,' we also believe and therefore speak" (2
Corinthians 4:13 NKJV).

Grace

Grace is a message that has been lost through time also in the
world today. The message of grace is very simple, but we have made
it complicated. Grace is the unmerited favor of God; we cannot do
anything ourselves to merit it, which is a gift from God: "For by
grace you have been saved through faith, and that not of yourselves;
it is the gift of God" (Ephesians 2:8 NKJV).

Many believers might not admit to it, but in their hearts, they
believe that without Jesus and the kingdom of God, they can still
succeed and prosper. By believing and walking this out daily, they
fall from kingdom authority and God's grace back into the law and

back into endeavoring to deserve and warrant achievement by their own efforts. If you can believe God for salvation by grace, you can also believe God for anything by grace. Grace is that special endowment upon the believer from God. Grace gives you access to everything that is pertaining to God and his kingdom. "Therefore, having been justified by faith, we have peace with God through our Lord Jesus Christ, through whom also we have access by faith into this grace in which we stand, and rejoice in hope of the glory of God" (Romans 5:1–2).

Justified once again means it's as if we had never sinned; we will have peace with God because of our relationship with our Lord Jesus Christ. We have access, *prosogoge*,[13] "the leading into something or the bringing into the presence of." Because of the grace in which we stand, we can rejoice in hope of the glory of God and his kingdom. The moment we repent and turn away from sin and back to God, we stand in grace. God's grace gives us immediate access to God's kingdom. We don't inherit eternal life by grace; there's more to it than that: "But, beloved, we are confident of better things concerning you, yes, things that accompany salvation, though we speak in this manner" (Hebrews 6:9 NKJV).

Grace makes the promises of God sure to all the seed of Abraham, the father of Faith. Christ has redeemed us from the curse of the Law and all its bondage so we might receive the promise of the spirit through faith. Christ redeems us; we are brought into a kingdom that is received by faith. Remember this! If you are of Christ, you are Abraham's seed and heir according to the promise.

One person constantly struggled with past sins and alienation from God. The enemies of God constantly badgered this person

---

[13] Vine's Complete Expository Dictionary of Old and New Testament Words (Publisher Thomas Nelson 1996)

with condemnation. The person believed that if he did church work or lived a moral life, he would inherit the kingdom. He thought that all would be well with his soul if he strove for perfection and good works. He worked long hours doing church work and not eating right. Lo and behold, when he died, he learned from Jesus that it didn't take all of that; all he had to do from day one was receive the kingdom of God as a little child through faith and according to God's grace. God's favor was there all the time; all he needed to do was take possession of it by faith and receive all that was his because of grace.

On another occasion, I was taken by the Spirit of God into a large warehouse-like building that was miles long. As I walked through this building, I saw rows and rows of packages neatly wrapped in golden paper. I asked my guide, the Holy Spirit, what these packages were. He said they were all the gifts and blessings of the kingdom that has gone unclaimed by believers on earth because of their lack of faith and not having walked in grace.

Go now and possess all that is yours because of grace. God wants you to have it all.

Conclusion

So while there are many views of the Kingdom circulating throughout the world today, the Holy Bible is absolutely clear in its presentation: The Kingdom of God is the rule or reign of God. The Kingdom of God is not the church, the Kingdom of God is not heaven, or moral reformation. The Kingdom of God is God's sovereignty in action against all the evil and unrighteousness in the world! While it is clear the Kingdom of God was the central theme of Jesus Christ teaching while here on earth, let us herald this message throughout the world today. It came into the world in Christ. It is both present and future. Its arrival, however, was startling. It came as a mystery, in an unexpected form through the humble person and work of Jesus as the Suffering Servant who defeated sin, death, and Satan. It has set us free! It is the fulfillment of the Old Testament promises of redemption and the covenants of God.

Even though it may seem as though the Kingdom of God is no longer reigning or ruling, since there is so much evil at work in the world today, let me be clear the existence of God's Kingdom is present and at work today. Evil will not triumph, nor will it prevail. In the end "A Real Kingdom is Coming" and it is certain to rule now in the present and also in the future. I pray that this writing has enlightened you in your continued evolution to be more like Christ.

Accept the Lord Jesus Christ today! Make him your Lord and Savior. If one shall enter the Kingdom of God, he must repent of his sins by turning away from sinful practices and stopping sin and turning his heart back towards God. Jesus Christ was clear when he proclaimed, "Repent, for the kingdom of heaven is at hand." (Matthew 4:17 (KJV) The Apostle Paul encouraged persons like this: "That if thou shalt confess with thy mouth the Lord Jesus, and shalt believe in thine heart that God hath raised him from the dead, thou shalt be saved. For with the heart man believeth unto righteousness; and with the mouth confession is made unto salvation." (Romans 10:9,10 KJV) You can accept the Lord Jesus Christ right now and ask him to come into your heart by praying this prayer today. Once you have allowed Jesus Christ to come into your heart you become a citizen of The Kingdom of God. Please pray this prayer today.

Prayer of Entrance in the Kingdom of God

"Lord Jesus Christ! I confess all my sins to you right now. I come into agreement with you today and I turn away from the practice of sin in my life. Lord Jesus Christ I now confess you as my Lord, Savior and King. Come into my heart today and abide there. Thank you Lord Jesus for accepting me into your Kingdom by Faith."

About the Author

Bishop Israel Marrone is a devout follower of Jesus Christ that is extremely dedicated to a life of prayer and the word of God. Bishop Israel Marrone was ordained in the Gospel Ministry in 1983. He has planted several churches throughout the country since that time. He is also passionate about the preservation of the Gospel of the Kingdom of God and Families. His primary concern in this hour is to lead the unchurched to Jesus Christ as their Lord and Savior. His goal is Reformation by restoring responsibility in people, credibility in churches, and civility in culture. He is a disciple, pastor, bishop, teacher, husband and entrepreneur.

As a Disciple, he has allowed the Holy Spirit to discipline him to teach and preach the central theme of Jesus teaching while here on the earth. The Gospel of the Kingdom of God.

As a Pastor, he founded Alllove Faith Church in Antioch CA., in 2010 with one family. Today, it is a church growing weekly in several locations in Northern CA, and this church has more than 10 community ministries to groups such as health, prisoner re-entry, addicts, single parents, and those with HIV/AIDS.

As a Bishop, he was consecrated by the Church of God in Christ International and presently oversees the California Pacific Ecclesiastical Jurisdiction. Seeing the need to train pastors and implement change to the overall church climate he oversees churches in Northern California in Oakland, Hayward, Sacramento,

Antioch, Fresno, Stockton and Vallejo. These church leaders meet monthly for hands on training and fellowship.

As a Teacher, he has authored the book titled Discipleship, a book on learning the life, teaching and practices of Jesus Christ

As a Husband, he is married to Shanda and from this relationship he is father to 3 children that serves diligently and faithfully in the ministry. LaMar, Justin and Brittany. He has many spiritual sons and daughters also. He often gives his testimony how God can restore families after tragic infidelity because God did it for him. God has kept this family together for over 30 years through many trials and test.

As an Entrepreneur, he is Vice President and Chief Operating Officer of OURTV television broadcasting Network located in Oakland CA

Bishop Israel Marrone is the present host of the daily television program "Another Day of Victory" world-wide on various networks.

Printed in the United States
By Bookmasters